MW01017196

Mental Chemistry

By the Author of

The Master Key System

REG. U. S.
PAT. OFF.

SAINT LOUIS, MO.

CHARLES F. HAANEL

1922-

COPYRIGHT 1922 BY

CHARLES F. HAANEL

ALL RIGHTS RESERVED.

Mental Chemistry

Man is Mind, and evermore
He takes the tool of thought
And, shaping what he wills,
Brings forth a thousand ills.
He thinks in secret and it comes to pass.
Environment is but his looking glass.

---James Allen.

CONTENTS

FIRST PRINTING DECEMBER, 1923
SECOND PRINTING JANUARY, 1923
THIRD PRINTING MAY, 1923

MENTAL CHEMISTRY

Chemistry is the science which treats of the intra-atomic or the intra-molecular changes which material things undergo under various influences.

Mental is defined as "of or appertaining to the mind, including intellect, feeling, and will, or the entire rational nature."

Science is knowledge gained and verified by exact observation and correct thinking.

Mental chemistry is, therefore, the science which treats of the changes which conditions undergo through the operations of the mind.

As the transformations which are brought about in applied chemistry are the result of the orderly combination of materials, it follows that mental chemistry brings about results in a like manner.

Any conceivable number may be formed with the arabic numerals 1, 2, 3, 4, 5, 6, 7, 8, 9, 0.

Any conceivable thought may be expressed with the 26 letters of the alphabet.

Any conceivable thing can be organized with the 14 elements and always and only by the proper grouping of electrons into molecules.

When two or more molecules are grouped a new individuality is created, and this individuality which has been called into being possesses characteristics which are not possessed by either of the elements which gave it being.

Thus one atom of sodium and one of chlorine give us salt, and this combination alone can give us salt, and no other combination of elements can give us salt, and salt is something very different from either of the elements of which it is composed.

What is true in the inorganic world is likewise true in the organic—certain conscious processes will produce certain effects, and the result will invariably be the same. The same thought will always be followed by the same consequence, and no other thought will serve the purpose.

This must necessarily be true because the principle must exist independently of the organs through which they function. Light must exist—otherwise there could be no eye. Sound must exist—otherwise there could be no ear. Mind must exist—otherwise there could be no brain.

Mental action is therefore the interaction of the individual upon the Universal Mind, and as the Universal Mind is the intelligence which pervades all space and animates all living things, this mental action and reaction is the law of causation.

It is the Universal Chemist, but the principle of causation does not obtain in the individual mind but in the Universal Mind. It is not an objective faculty but a subjective process.

The individual may, however, bring the power into manifestation and as the possible combinations of thought are infinite, the results are seen in an infinite variety of conditions and experiences.

Primordial man, naked and bestial, squatting in gloomy caverns, gnawing bones, was born, lived, and died in a hostile world. His hostility and his wretchedness arose from his ignorance. His hand-maidens were Hate and Fear. His sole reliance was his club. He saw in the beasts, forests, torrents, seas, clouds, and even in his fellow man, only enemies. He recognized no ties binding them one to another or to himself.

Modern man is born to comparative luxury. Love rocks his cradle and shields his youth. When he goes forth to struggle he wields a pencil, not a club. He relies upon his brain, not his brawn. He knows the physical as neither master nor equal, but as a useful servant. His fellow men and the forces of Nature are his friends—not his enemies.

These tremendous changes, from hate to love, from fear to confidence, from material strife to mental control, have been wrought by the slow dawn of Understanding. In direct proportion as he understands Cosmic Law is man's lot enviable or the reverse.

Thought builds organic structures in animals and men. The protoplasmic cell desires the light and sends forth its impulse; this impulse gradually builds an eye. A species of deer feed in a country where the leaves grow on high branches, and the constant reaching for their favorite food builds cell by cell the neck of the giraffe. The amphibian reptiles desire to fly in the open air above the water; they develop wings and become birds.

Experiments with parasites found on plants indicate that even the lowest order of life makes use of mental chemistry. Jacques Loeb, M. D., Ph. D., a member of the Rockefeller Institute made the following experiment: "In order to obtain the material, potted rose bushes are brought into a room and placed in front of a closed window. If the plants are allowed to dry out, the aphides (parasites), previously wingless, change to winged insects. After the metamorphosis, the insects leave the plants, fly to the window and then creep upward on the glass.''

It is evident that these tiny insects found that the plants on which they had been thriving were dead, and that they could therefore secure nothing more to eat and drink from this source. The only method by which they could save themselves from starvation was to grow temporary wings and fly, which they did.

That the brain cells are directly affected by mental pictures, and that the brain cells in their turn can affect the entire being, was proven by Prof. Elmer Gates of the Smithsonian Institution at Washington. Guinea pigs were kept in enclosures with certain colors dominant; dissection showed their brains to be larger in the color area than those of the same class of guinea pigs kept in other inclosures. The perspiration of men in various mental moods was analyzed, and the resultant salts experimented with. Those of a man in an angry state were of an unusual color; a small portion put on the tongue of a dog produced evidences of poisoning.

Experiments at Harvard College with students on the weighing board proved that the mind moves the blood. When the student was told to imagine that he was running a foot race, the board sank down at the foot, and when a problem in mathematics was being worked the balanced board sank down at the head.

This shows that thought not only flashes constantly between mind and mind, with an intensity and swiftness far transcending electricity, but that it also builds the structures through which it operates.

Through the conscious mind we know ourselves as individuals, and take cognizance of the world about us. The subconscious mind is the storehouse of past thoughts.

We can understand the action of the conscious and subconscious minds by observing the process by which the child learns to play the piano. He is taught how to hold his hands and strike the keys, but at first he finds it somewhat difficult to control the movement of his fingers. He must practice daily, must concentrate his thoughts upon his fingers, consciously making the right movements. These thoughts, in time, become subconscious, and the fingers are directed and controlled in the playing by the subconsciousness. In his first months, and possibly first years of practice, the pupil can perform only by keeping his conscious mind centered upon the work; but later he can play with ease and at the same time carry on a conversation with those about him, because the subconscious has become so thoroughly imbued with the idea of right movements that it can direct them without demanding the attention of the conscious mind.

The subconscious is instinctive desire. It carries out what is suggested by the conscious mind. These suggestions it carries out faithfully, and it is this close relation between the conscious and subconscious which makes conscious thinking so important.

Man's organism is controlled by the subconscious thought; circulation, breathing, digestion, and assimilation are all activities controlled by the subconscious. The subconscious is continually getting its impulses from the conscious, and we have only to change our conscious thought to get a corresponding change in the subconscious.

We live in a fathomless sea of plastic mind substance. This substance is ever alive and active. It is sensitive to the highest degree. It takes form according to the mental demand. Thought forms the mould or matrix from which the substance expresses. Our ideal is the mould from which our future will emerge.

The Universe is alive. In order to express life there must be mind; nothing can exist without mind. Everything which exists is some manifestation of this one basic substance from which and by which all things have been created and are continually being recreated. It is man's capacity to think that makes him a creator instead of a creature.

All things are the result of the thought process. Man has accomplished the seemingly impossible because he has refused to consider it impossible. By concentration men have made the connection between the finite and the Infinite, the limited and the Unlimited, the visible and the Invisible, the personal and the Impersonal. _INDIVIDUAL / UNIVERSAL_

Great musicians have succeeded in thrilling the world by the creation of divine rhapsodies. Great inventors have made the connection and startled the world by their wonderful creations. Great authors, great philosophers, great scientists have secured this harmony to such an extent that though their writings were created hundreds of years ago, we are just beginning to realize their truth. Love of music, love of business, love of creation caused these people to concentrate, and the ways and means of materializing their ideals slowly but surely developed.

Throughout the entire Universe the law of cause and effect is ever at work. This law is supreme; here a cause, there an effect. They can never operate independently. One is supplementary to the other. Nature at all times is endeavoring to establish a perfect equilibrium. This is the law of the Universe and is ever active. Universal harmony is the goal for which all nature strives. The entire cosmos moves under this law. The sun, the moon, the stars are all held in their respective positions because of harmony. They travel their orbits, they appear at certain times in certain places, and because of the precision of this law, astronomers are able to tell us where various stars will appear in a thousand years. The scientist bases his entire hypothesis on this law of cause and effect. Nowhere is it held in dispute except in the domain of man. Here we find people speaking of luck, chance, accident, and mishap; but is any one of these possible? Is the Universe a unit? If so, and there is law and order in one part, it must extend throughout all parts. This is a scientific deduction.

Like begets like on every plane of existence, and while people believe this more or less vaguely, they refuse to give it any consideration where they are concerned. This is due to the fact that heretofore man could never realize how he set certain causes in motion which related him with his various experiences.

It is only in the past few years that a working hypothesis could be formulated to apply this law to man—the goal of the Universe is harmony. This means a perfect balance between all things.

Ether fills all interplanetary space. This more or less metaphysical substance is the elementary basis of all matter. It is upon this substance that the messages of the wireless are transmitted through space.

Thought dropped into this substance causes vibrations which in turn unite with similar vibrations and react upon the thinker. All manifestations are the result of thought—but the thinking is on different planes.

We have one plane of thought constituting the animal plane. Here are actions and interactions which animals respond to, yet men know nothing of. Then we have the conscious thought plane. Here are almost limitless planes of thought to which man may be responsive. It is strictly the nature of our thinking that determines to which plane we shall respond. On this plane, we have the thoughts of the ignorant, the wise, the poor, the wealthy, the sick, the healthy, the very poor, the very rich, and so on. The number of thought planes is infinite, but the point is that when we think on a definite plane, we are responsive to thoughts on that plane, and the effect of the reaction is apparent in our environment.

Take for example one who is thinking on the thought plane of wealth. He is inspired with an idea, and the result is success. It could not be otherwise. He is thinking on the success plane, and as like attracts like, his thoughts attract other similar thoughts, all of which contribute to his success. His receiver is attuned for success thoughts only, all other messages fail to reach his consciousness, hence, he knows nothing of them; his antennæ, as it were, reach into the Universal Ether and connect with the ideas by which his plans and ambitions may be realized.

Sit right where you are, place an amplifier to your ear, and you may hear the most beautiful music, or a lecture, or the latest market reports. What does this indicate, in addition to the pleasure derived from the music or the information received from the lecture or market reports?

It indicates first that there must be some substance sufficiently refined to carry these vibrations to every part of the world. Again it indicates that this substance must be sufficiently refined to penetrate every other substance known to man. The vibrations must penetrate wood, brick, stone or steel of any kind. They must go over, through and under rivers, mountains, above the earth, under the earth, everywhere and anywhere. Again it indicates that time and space have been annihilated. The instant a piece of music is broadcasted in Pittsburgh or anywhere else, by putting the proper mechanism to your ear you can get it as clearly and distinctly as though you were in the same room. This indicates that these vibrations proceed in every direction; wherever there is an ear to hear, it may hear.

If then there is a substance so refined that it will take up the human voice, and send it in every direction so that every human being who is equipped with the proper mechanism may receive the message, is it not possible that the same substance will carry a thought just as readily and just as certainly? Most assuredly. How do we know this? By experimentation. This is the only way to be certain of anything. Try it. Make the experiment yourself.

Sit right where you are. Select a subject with which you are fairly familiar. Begin to think. The thoughts will follow each other in rapid succession. One thought will suggest another. You will soon be surprised at some of the thoughts which have made you a channel of their manifestation. You did not know that you knew so much about the subject. You did not know that you could put them into such beautiful language. You marvel at the ease and rapidity with which the thoughts arrive. Where do they come from? From the One Source of all wisdom, all power, and all understanding. You have been to the source of all knowledge, for every thought which has ever been thought is still in existence, ready and waiting for someone to attach the mechanism by which it can find expression. You can therefore think the thoughts of every sage, every artist, every financier, every captain of industry who ever existed, for thoughts never die.

Suppose your experiment is not entirely successful; try again. Few of us are proud of our first effort at anything. We did not even make a very great success in trying to walk the first time we tried. If you try again, remember that the brain is the organ of the objective mind, that it is related to the objective world by the cere-bro-spinal or voluntary nervous system; that this system of nerves is connected with the objective world by certain mech-anism or senses. These are the organs with which we see, hear, feel, taste, and smell. Now, a thought is a thing which can neither be seen, nor heard; we cannot taste it, nor can we smell it, nor can we feel it. Evi-dently the five senses can be of no possible value in trying to receive a thought. They must therefore be stilled, because thought is a spiritual activity and cannot reach us through any material channel. We will then relax both mentally and physically and send out an S. O. S. for help and await the result. The success of our experiment will then depend entirely upon our ability to become receptive.

Scientists like to make use of the word Ether in speaking of the substance "In which we live and move and have our be-ing," which is Omnipresent, which impen-etrates everything, and which is the source of all activity. They like to use the word

Ether because Ether implies something which can be measured and so far as the materialistic school of scientists is concerned, anything which cannot be measured does not exist; but who can measure an electron? And yet the electron is the basis for all material existence, so far as we know at present.

It would require 500,000,000 atoms placed side by side to measure one linear inch. A number of atoms equal to twenty-five million times the population of the earth must be present in the test tube for a chemist to detect them in a chemical trace. About 125 septillions of atoms are in an inch cube of lead. And we cannot come anywhere near even seeing an atom through a microscope!

Yet the atom is as large as our solar system compared to the electrons of which it is composed. All atoms are alike in having one positive central sun of energy around which one or more negative charges of energy revolve. The number of negative electrons each atom contains determines the nature of the so-called "element" of which it is a part.

An atom of hydrogen, for instance, is supposed to have one negative electron as a satellite to its positive center. For this reason chemists accept it as a standard of atomic weight. The atomic weight of hydrogen is placed at 1.

The diameter of an electron is to the diameter of the atom as the diameter of our Earth is to the diameter of the orbit in which it moves around the sun. More specifically, it has been determined that an electron is one-eighteen-thousandth of the mass of a hydrogen atom.

It is clear therefore that matter is capable of a degree of refinement almost beyond the power of the human mind to calculate. We have not as yet been able to analyze this refinement beyond the electron, and even in getting thus far have had to supplement our physical observation of effects with imagination to cover certain gaps.

The building up of Matter from Electrons has been an involuntary process of individualizing intelligent energy.

Food, water and air are usually considered to be the three essential elements necessary to sustain life. This is very true, but there is something still more essential. Every time we breathe we not only fill our lungs with air which has been charged with magnetism by the Solar Orb, but we fill ourselves with Pranic Energy, the breath of life replete with every requirement for mind and spirit. This life giving spirit is far more necessary than air, food, or water, because a man can live for forty days without food, for three days without water, and for a few minutes without air; but he cannot live a single second without Ether. It is the one prime essential of life, and contains all the essentials of life, so that the process of breathing furnishes not only food for body building, but food for mind and spirit as well.

THE CHEMIST

Universal intelligence leaves its source to become embodied in material forms through which it returns to its source as an individual or entity. Mineral life animated by electro-magnetism is the first step of intelligence upward, toward its universal source. Universal energy is intelligent, and this involuntary process by which matter is built up, is an intelligent process of nature which has for its specific purpose the individualization of her intelligence.

Stockwell says: "The basis of life and consciousness lies back of the atoms, and may be found in the universal ether." Hemstreet says: "Mind in the ether is no more unnatural than mind in flesh and blood." Stockwell says: "The ether is coming to be apprehended as an immaterial superphysical substance, filling all space, carrying in its infinite, throbbing bosom the specks of aggregated dynamic

27

force called worlds. It embodies the ultimate spiritual principle, and represents the
unity of those forces and energies from
which spring, as their source, all phenomena, physical, mental, and spiritual, as
they are known to man.'' Dolbear, in his
great work on ether, says: ''Besides
the function of energy and motion, the
ether has other inherent properties, out
of which could emerge, under proper circumstances, other phenomena, such as life
or mind or whatever may be in the sub-
stratum.''

The microscopic cell, a minute speck of
matter that is to become man, has in it the
promise and germ of mind. May we not
draw the inference that the elements of
mind are present in those chemical elements—carbon, oxygen, hydrogen, nitrogen, sulphur, phosphorous, sodium, potassium, chlorine—that are found in the cell?
Not only must we do so; but we must go
further, since we know that each of these
elements, and every other, is built up of
one invariable unit, the electron, and we

must therefore assert that mind is potential in the unit of matter—the electron itself.''

Atoms of mineral matter are attracted to each other to form aggregates or masses. This attraction is called Chemical Affinity. Chemical combinations of atoms are due to their magnetic relations to each other. Positive atoms will always attract negative atoms. The combination will last only so long as a still more positive force is not brought to bear on it to break it apart.

Two or more atoms brought into combination form a molecule, which is defined as ''the smallest particle of a substance that can maintain its own identity.'' Thus a molecule of water is a combination of two atoms of hydrogen and one atom of oxygen (H_2O).

In building a plant, nature works with colloid cells rather than with atoms, for she has built up the cell as an entity just as she built the atom and the molecule as entities with which to work in mineral substance. The vegetable cell (colloid), has power to draw to itself from earth, air, and water whatever energies it needs for its growth. It therefore draws from mineral life and dominates it.

When vegetable matter is sufficiently refined to be receptive to still more of the universal intelligent energy, animal life appears. The plant cells have now become so plastic that they have additional capacities—those of individual consciousness, and also additional powers; those of sensational magnetism. It draws its life forces from both mineral and plant life, and therefore dominates them.

The body is an aggregate of cells animated by the spiritual magnetic life that tends toward organizing these cells into communities, and these communities into co-ordinated bodies which will operate the entire mass of the body as a conscious entity able to carry itself from one place to the other.

Atoms and molecules and their energies are now subordinated to the welfare of the cell. Each cell is a living, conscious entity, capable of selecting its own food, of resisting aggression, and of reproducing itself.

As each cell has its individual consciousness, intuition, and volition, so each federated group of cells has a collective individual consciousness, intuition, and volition. Likewise, each co-ordinated group of federations; until the entire body has one central brain where the great co-ordination of all the "brains" takes place.

The body of an average human being is composed of some twenty-six trillions (26,-000,000,000,000) of cells; the brain and the spinal cord by themselves consist of some two billion.

The biogenic law proves that every vertebrate, like every other animal, evolves from a single cell. Even the human organism, according to Haeckel, is at first a simple nucleated globule of plasm, about 1.125 inch in diameter, barely visible to the naked eye as a tiny point. The ovum transmits to the child by heredity the personal traits of the mother, the sperm-cell those of the father; and this hereditary transmission extends to the finest characteristics of the soul as well as the body. What is plasm? What is this mysterious living substance that we find everywhere as the material foundation of the wonders of life? Plasm or protoplasm, is, as Huxley rightly said, the physical basis of organic life; to speak more precisely, it is a chemical compound of carbon that alone accomplishes the various processes of life. In its simplest form the living cell is merely a soft globule of plasm, containing a firmer nucleus. As soon as it is fertilized, it multiplies by division and forms a community or colony of many special cells.

These differentiate themselves, and by their specialization, or modifications, the tissues which compose the various organs are developed. The developed, many-celled organisms of man and all higher animals resemble, a social, civil community, the numerous single individuals of which are developed in various ways, but were originally only simple cells of one common structure.

All life on this earth, as Dr. Butler points out in "How the Mind Cures," began in the form of a cell which consisted of a body animated by a mind. In the beginning and long afterward the animating mind was the one we now call the subconscious. But as the forms grew in complexity and produced organs of sense, the mind threw out an addition, . . . forming another part, the one we now call the conscious. While at first all living creatures had but one guide that they must follow in all things, this later addition to mind gave the creature a choice. This was the formation of what has been termed Free Will."

Each cell is endowed with an individual intelligence, that helps it carry on, as by a miracle, its complex labours. The cell is the basis of man, and this fact must be constantly borne in mind in dealing with the wonders of mental chemistry.

As a nation is made up of a large number of living individuals, so the body is made up of a large number of living cells. The citizens of a country are engaged in varied pursuits—some in the work of production, in field, forest, mine, factory; some in the work of distribution, in transportation, in warehouse, store, or bank; some in the work of regulation, in legislative halls, on the bench, in the executive chair; some in the work of protection—soldiers, sailors, doctors, teachers, preachers. Likewise in the body some cells are working on production: mouth, stomach, intestines, lungs, supplying food, water, air; some are engaged in distribution of supplies and elimination of wastes: heart, blood, lymph, lungs, liver, kidneys, skin; some perform the office of regulation: brain, spinal cord, nerves; some are occupied in protection; white blood corpuscles, skin, bone, muscle; there are also cells to which are entrusted the reproduction of species.

As the vigour and welfare of a nation depend fundamentally on the vitality and efficiency and co-operation of its citizens, so the health and life of the body depend upon the vitality, efficiency and co-operation of its myriad cells.

We have seen that the cells are gathered into systems and groups for the performance of particular functions essential to physical life and expression, such as we see in organs and tissues.

So long as the several parts all act together, in concord and due regard to one another and the general purposes of the organism, there is health and efficiency. But when from any cause discord arises, illness supervenes. Disease is lack of comfort and harmony.

In the brain and nervous system the cells are grouped in their action according to the particular functions which they are called upon to perform. It is in this way that we are able to see, to taste, to smell, to feel, and to hear. It is also in this way we are able to recall past experiences, to remember facts and figures, and so on.

In mental and physical health these various groups of neurons work in fine harmony, but in dis-ease they do not. In normal conditions the ego holds all these individual cells and groups, as well as system of cells, in harmonious and co-ordinate action.

Disease represents dissociated organic action; certain systems or groups, each of which is made up of a vast number of microscopic cells, begin functioning independently, and hence inharmoniously; and thus upset the tone of the whole organism. A single organ or system can thus get out of tune with the rest of the body and do serious harm. This is one kind of disease.

In a federation of any sort, efficiency and concord of action depend upon the strength and confidence accorded the central administration of its affairs; and just in proportion to the degree of failure to maintain these conditions are discord and confusion sure to ensue.

Nels Quevli makes this clear in "Cell Intelligence." He says, "The intelligence of man is the intelligence possessed by the cells in his brain. If man is intelligent and by virtue thereof is able to combine and arrange matter and force so as to effect structures, such as houses and railroads, why is not the cell also intelligent when he is able to direct the forces of nature so as to effect the structures we see such as plants and animals. The cell is not compelled to act by reason of any chemical and mechanical force, any more than is man. He acts by reason of will and judgment of his own. He is a separate living animal. Bergson in his ''Creative Evolution'' seems to see in matter and life a creative energy. If we stood at a distance watching a skyscraper gradually grow into completeness, we would say there must be some creative energy back of it, pushing the construction and, if we could never get near enough to see the men and builders at work, we could have no other idea of how that skyscraper came into existence except that it was caused by some creative energy.

The cell is an animal, very highly organized and specialized. Take the single cell called amœba for instance. He has no machinery with which he can manufacture starch. He does, however, carry with

him building material with which he can
in an emergency save his life by covering
himself with a coat of armor. Other cells
carry with them a structure which is called
chromatophore. With this instrument,
these cells are able to manufacture starch
from the crude substances of earth, air and
water by the aid of sunlight. From these
facts, it must appear evident to the reader
that the cell is a very highly organized and
specialized individual, and that to look at
him from the point of view of being mere
matter and force is the same as to compare the actions of a stone rolling down
a hill with that of an automobile moving
over a smooth pavement. One is compelled to move by reason of the force of
gravitation, while the other moves by virtue of the intellect that guides it. The
structures of life, like plants and animals,
are built from the materials taken from the
earth, air, and water, just as are the structures man builds, like railroads and sky-
scrapers. If we were asked how it is possible for man to effect the construction of

these railroads and buildings, we would say
that it is by reason of the fact that he is
an intelligent being.

If the cell has gone through the same
process of social organization and evolution as man, why is it not also the same intelligent being as man? Did you ever stop
to think what takes place when the surface of the body is cut or bruised? The
white blood cells or corpuscles, as they are
called, who are the general caretakers of
the body, whose duty it is to look after
everything in general, such as the fighting of
bacteria and disease germs and the general
repair work, will sacrifice their own lives
by thousands if necessary to save the body.
They live in the body, enjoying complete
liberty. They do not float in the blood
stream except when in a hurry to get somewhere, but move around everywhere as
separate independent beings to see that
everything goes right. If a bruise or cut
happens, they are at once informed, and
rush to the spot by thousands and direct
the repair work and if necessary they

change their own occupation and take a different job, that of making connective tissue in order to bind the tissues together. In nearly every open sore, bruise or cut, they are killed in great numbers in their faithful effort to repair and close up the wound. A text book on physiology briefly speaks of it as follows:

"When the skin is injured the white blood cells form new tissue upon the surface, while the epithelium spreads over it from the edges, stopping the growth and completing the healing processes."

There seems to be no particular center in the body around which intelligence revolves. Every cell seems to be a center of intelligence and knows what its duties are wherever it is placed and wherever we find it. Every citizen of the cell republic is an intelligent independent existence, and all are working together for the welfare of all. Nowhere can we find more absolute sacrifice of the lives of the individuals to the general welfare of all than we do in the cell republic. The results cannot be obtained in any other way nor at any less cost of individual sacrifice, so it is necessary to their social existence. The principle of individual sacrifice to common welfare has been accepted and agreed upon as the right thing and as their common duty, impartially distributed among them, and they perform their allotted work and duties regardless of their own individual comfort.

Mr. Edison says, "I believe that our bodies are made up of myraids of units of life. Our body is not itself the unit of life or a unit of life. Let me give you as an example the S. S. Mauretania.

"The 'Mauretania' is not herself a living thing—it is the men in her that are alive. If she is wrecked on the coast, for instance, the men get out, and when the men get out it simply means that the 'life units' leave the ship. And so in the same way a man is not 'dead' because his body is buried and the vital principle, that is, the 'life units,' have left the body.

"Everything that pertains to life is still

<u>living and cannot be destroyed.</u> Everything that pertains to life is still subject to the laws of animal life. We have myriads of cells and it is the inhabitants in these cells, inhabitants which themselves are beyond the limits of the microscope, which vitalize our body.

"To put it in another way, I believe that these life-units of which I have spoken band themselves together in countless millions and billions in order to make a man. We have too facilely assumed that each one of us is himself a unit. This, I am convinced is wrong, even by the high-powered microscope, and so we have assumed that the unit is the man, which we can see, and have ignored the existence of the real life units, which are those we cannot see.

"No man today can set the line as to where 'life' begins and ends. Even in the formation of crystals, we see a definitely ordered plan of work. Certain solutions will always form a particular kind of crystal without variation. It is not impossible that these life entities are at work in the mineral and plant as in what we call the 'animal' world.''

We have seen something of the chemist, something of his laboratory, something of his system of communication.

What about the product? This is a very practical age, an age of commercialism, if you please. If the chemist produces nothing of value, nothing which can be converted into cash, we are not interested.

But, fortunately the chemist in this case produces an article which has the highest cash value of any article known to man.

He provides the one thing which all the world demands, something which can be realized upon anywhere, at any time; it is not a slow asset; on the contrary, its value is recognized in every market.

The product is thought; thought rules the world; thought rules every Government, every bank, every industry, every person and everything in existence, and is differentiated from everything else, simply and only because of thought.

Every person is what he is because of his method of thinking, and men and nations differ from each other only because they think differently.

What then is thought? Thought is the product of the chemical laboratory possessed by every thinking individual; it is the blossom, the combined intelligence which is the result of all previous thinking processes; it is the fruit and contains the best of all that the individual has to give.

There is nothing material about a thought, and yet no man would give up his ability to think for all the gold in Christendom; it is therefore of more value than anything which exists. As it is not material it must be spiritual. Here then is an explanation of the wonderful value of thought. Thought is a spiritual activity; in fact, it is the only activity which the spirit possesses. Spirit is the creative principle of the Universe, as a part must be the same in kind and quality as the whole, and can differ only in degree, thought must be creative also.

THE LABORATORY.

The art of chemistry cannot proceed without a plant, or work-shop, and one of the most interesting features of the human system is its series of manufacturing plants in which are produced the chemical agents necessary to mobilize the constitutents of food. And it is a part of the fine natural economy that the secretions containing these chemical agents should serve several other purposes also. In general, each may be said to have an alterative effect upon the others, or at least upon the activities of the other plants; also they act upon the inwardbound nerve paths as exciters of effects in both the conscious and the subconscious activities.

Radiant energy, whether consciously or subconsciously released from the body, becomes the medium of sensory impressions that flash back to the perceptive centers and there set up reactions which are interpreted by these centers according to their stage of development of self, and therefore they interpret these messages exactly as they are received, without attempt to "think" about them, or to analyze them. The process is as mechanical as an impression made by the actinic rays of the sun on a photographic plate.

The general principle by which an idea is preserved is vibratory like all other phenomena of nature. Every thought causes vibrations that will continue to expand and contract in wave circles, like the waves started by a stone dropped in a pool of water. Waves from other thoughts may counteract it, or it may finally succumb of its own inanition.

Thought will instantly set in motion the finest of spiritual magnetism, and this motion will be communicated to the heavier and coarser densities, and will eventually affect the physical matter of the body.

Life is not created—it simply IS. All nature is animate with this force we call "life." The phenomena of life on this physical plane, with which we are chiefly concerned, are produced by the involution of "energy" into "matter," and matter is, itself, an involution of energy.

But when the stage of matter is reached in the process of Nature's involution, matter then begins to evolve forms under the action upon it and within it. So that growth and life are the results of a simultaneous integration of matter and energy. Evolution starts with the lowest form of matter, and works upward through refining processes to serve as a matrix of energy.

The internal secretions constitute and determine much of the inherited powers of the individual and their development. They control physical and mental growth, and all the metabolic processes of fundamental importance. They dominate all the vital functions of man. They co-operate in an intimate relationship which may be compared to an interlocking directorate. A derangement of their functions, causing an insufficiency of them, an excess or an abnormality upsets the entire equilibrium of the body, with transformed effect upon the mind and the organs. Blood chemistry of our time is a marvel undreamed of a generation ago.

These achievements are a perfect example of accomplished fact contradicting all former prediction and criticism. One of the greatest advances of modern medicine has been the study of the processes and secretions of the hitherto obscure ductless glands; endocrinology, as this study is called, has thrown much valuable light upon certain abnormal physical conditions about which science had until now been in the dark. We now know that most of the freaks of nature we see on exhibition are such owing to endocrine disturbance—the disturbance of the ductless glands. The bearded lady, a victim of pogoniasis; the victims of obesity and of skeletonization; of acromegalis, or giantism; of micromegalia or liliputianism—all such evolutional deviations are due to subnormalities or abnormalities of the chemical elements which the glands produce and send into the blood-stream.

These are no mere theories, for they have been rigorously tested in the laboratories of science. As Sir William Osler, one of the world's most illustrious luminaries of knowledge, has said: "For man's body, too, is a humming hive of working cells, each with its specific function, all under central control of the brain and heart, and all dependent on materials called hormones (secreted by small, even insignificant looking structures) which lubricate the wheels of life. For example, remove the thyroid gland just below the adam's apple, and you deprive man of the lubricants which enable his thought-engines to work. It is as if you cut off the oil-supply of a motor, and gradually the stored acquisitions of his mind cease to be available, and within a year he sinks into dementia. The normal processes of the skin cease, the hair falls, the features bloat, and the paragon of animals is transformed into a shapeless caricature of humanity."

These essential lubricators, of which a number are now known, are called harmones—you will recognize from its derivation how appropriate is the term. The name is derived from the Greek verb meaning "to rouse or set in motion." The name was given by Starling and Bayliss, two great Englishmen noted for their research work in endocrinology. Cretins—dwarfed imbeciles—can be cured by the administration, internally, of the thyroid glands of sheep, with truly miraculous results; because cretinism is caused by the lack or absence of thyroid gland secretions.

As an instance of the fascination of these studies, consider the conception that the thyroid played a fundamental part in the change of sea creatures into land animals. Feeding the Mexican axolotl, a purely aquatic newt, breathing through gills, on thyroid, quickly changes it into the ambystoma, a terrestrial salamander, breathing by means of lungs.

The endocrine glands produce secretions which enter the blood-stream and vitally affect the bodily structure and functions.

The pituitary is a small gland, located near the center of the head, directly under the third ventricle of the brain, where it rests in a depression in the bony floor-plate of the skull. Its secretions have an important part in the mobilizing of carbo-hydrates, maintaining blood-pressure, stimulating other glands, and maintaining the tonicity of the sympathetic nerve system. Its under, or over, activity during childhood, will produce marked characteristics in the body structure, and what concerns us more, equally marked characteristics of mental development and function.

The thyroid gland is located at the frontal base of the neck, extending upward in a sort of semicircle on both sides, with the parathyroids near the tips. The thyroid secretion is important in mobilizing both proteids and carbohydrates; it stimulates other glands, helps resist infections, affects the hair growth, and influences the organs of digestion and elimination. It is a strongly determining factor in the all-around physical development, and also in the mental functioning. A well-balanced thyroid goes a long way toward insuring an active, efficient, smoothly co-ordinated mind and body.

The adrenal glands are located just above the small of the back. These organs have been called by some writers the "decorative glands," since one of their functions appears to be that of keeping the pigments of the body in proper solution and distribution. But of greater importance is the agency of the adrenal secretion in other directions. It contains a most valuable blood-pressure agent; it is a tonic to the sympathetic nerve system, hence to the involuntary muscles, heart, arteries, intestines, and so on; as well as to the perceptive paths. It responds to certain emotional excitements by an immediate increase in volume of secretion, thus increasing the energy of the whole system, and preparing it for effective response.

The cerebro-spinal nervous system is the telephone system of the conscious mind; it is a very complete wiring system for communication from the brain to every part of the body, especially the terminals. It is the intelligence department of self-conscious man.

The sympathetic nervous system is the system of the subconscious mind. Behind the stomach, and in front of the spine, is the center of the system known as the "Solar Plexus." It is composed of two masses of brain substance, each in the shape of a crescent. They surround an artery whose function it is to equalize the blood pressure of all the abdominal organs.

Just as the brain and the voluntary nervous system constitute the apparatus of self-conscious man, in like manner the solar plexus and the sympathetic system comprise the special apparatus of the subconscious mind.

The function of the sympathetic nervous system is to maintain the equilibrium of the body, to act as a balance wheel, to prevent over or under action of the cerebrospinal system. As it is directly affected by emotional states such as fear, anger, jealousy or hatred, these may easily throw out of gear the operation of the automatic functions of the body. That is to say, that emotional states such as joy, fear, anger and hatred may upset such functions of the body as digestion, blood circulation, general nutrition, and so forth.

"Nerves," and all the unpleasant experiences that follow in the way of bodily discomfort and ill health, are caused by negative emotions, such as fear, anger, hatred and the like; they break down the resistance which has been offered by the various plexii which, when in normal working order, have a definite capacity to inhibit the effect of such emotions.

The sympathetic system is the apparatus whose function it is to maintain the body in a normal and healthy working order, and to replace the wastage due to ordinary wear and tear, both emotional and physical. The kind of emotions which we entertain is therefore of great importance; if positive, they are constructive; if negative, they are destructive.

ATTRACTION

Mental chemistry is a power which is sweeping through eternity, a living stream of relative action in which the basic principle is ever active; it embraces the past and carries it forward into the ever widening future; a movement where relative action, cause, and effect go hand in hand; where law dovetails into law and where all laws are the ever willing handmaids of this great creative force.

This power stretches beyond the utmost planets, beyond a beginning, beyond an ending, and on into a beginningless and endless eternity; it causes the things we see to take form and shape. It brings the fruit from the blossom and the sweetness to the honey; it measures the sweep of the countless orbs; it lurks in the sparkle of the diamond, and in the amethyst and in the grape; it works in the seen and in the unseen, and it permeates the all.

It is the source of perfect justice, perfect unity, perfect harmony, and perfect truth, while its constant activity brings perfect balance, perfect growth, and perfect understanding.

Perfect justice, because it renders equal retribution.

Perfect unity, because it has oneness of purpose.

Perfect harmony, because in it all laws blend.

Perfect truth, because it is the one great truth of all existence.

Perfect balance, because it measures unerringly.

Perfect growth, because it is a natural growth.

Perfect understanding, because it solves every problem of life.

The reality of this law lies in its activity, for only through action, and constant change, can this law come to be; and only through inaction can it cease to be; but as there is no inaction, there can be no cessation.

The one purpose of this law is unchangeable; in the silence of darkness, in the glory of light, in the turmoil of action and the pain of reaction, it moves ever forward toward the fulfillment of its one great purpose—perfect harmony.

We see and feel its urge in the myriads and myriads of plant forms on hill and in dale, as they push forth from the same darkness into one light; and though bathed by the same waters and breathed upon by same air, yet all varieties maintain their own individuality—that is, the rose is always a rose and differs from the violet, which is always a violet; the acorn gives to the world the oak and never a willow or any other variety of tree; and though all send out roots into the same soil, and blossom in the same sunshine, yet some are frail, some are strong, some are bitter, and some are sweet; while others are repulsive, some are beautiful; thus all varieties draw to themselves through their own roots and from the same elements, that which differentiates them from each other; and this great law of life, this constant urge, this hidden force in the plant causing it to manifest, to grow, and to attain, is this Law of Attraction bearing forward in silent majesty, bringing all fruition; dictating nothing, yet making each unit of growth true to its own individual nature.

In the Mineral world it is the cohesion in the rock, sand, and clay; it is the strength in the granite, the beauty in the marble, the sparkle in the sapphire, and the blood in the ruby.

Thus do we find it working in the things we see; but its unseen power, as it works in the mind of man, is greater.

This Law of Attraction is neither good nor evil, neither moral nor immoral; it is a neutral law that always flows in conjunction with the desires of the individual; we each choose our own line of growth, and there are as many lines of growth as there are individuals; and although no two of us are exactly alike, yet many of us move along similar lines.

These lines of growth are made up of past, present, and future desires, manifesting in the ever forming present, where they establish the central line of our being along which we advance; the nature of these desires has no power to check the action of this, for its function is to bring to maturity the bitter as well as the sweet.

An illustration of the neutrality and action of this law is found in the grafting of an apple tree bud into a wild crab tree, where we find in due time eatable and uneatable fruits growing together on the same tree; that is, wholesome and unwholesome fruits nourished and brought to maturity by the same sap.

In applying this illustration to ourselves, we find that the cultured apples and the wild crabs represent our different desires, while the sap represents this Law of Growth; and just as the sap brings to maturity the different kinds of fruit, just so will this Law bring to fruitfulness our different kinds of desires; and whether they

be wholesome or unwholesome, it matters
not to the law, for its place in life is to
bring to our minds a conscious realization
of the results that follow all desires we
hold, as well as of their nature, their effect
and their purpose.

In man's division of the Law, we come
in contact with a larger activity, one that
is utterly unknown to the primitive mind,
which leads us to a conscious awakening
of a newer power in a larger field of action
—in other words, a larger truth, a greater
understanding, and a deeper insight.

We are touching a greater reality, for let
us understand that reality lies in activity
and not outside of it; to exist is to be alive
to the action of the laws about us; the hidden urge in the plant is its reality, and not
the outer form we see.

True knowledge comes to us through
our own activities, borrowed knowledge
through the activities of others; both together evolves our intellects. And slowly
we are forming an unique self, an individualizing unit.

As we move out into the power of our growing intellects, into an ever moving consciousness we are learning to seek for the wherefore and why of things, and in this search we think and imagine that we are original, when in fact we are only students of established beliefs, notions, and facts, gathered throughout generations of tribal and national life.

We live in a state of fear and uncertainty, until we find, and make use of, the unvarying uniformity running through all laws; this is a central truth that we must know and use before we can become masters of self, or masters of conditions. The Law of Growth ripens collectively, for its one function is: "to act upon that which we give it to act upon."

As the nature of the cause governs the effect, so does thought precede and predetermine action. Each one must use this Law knowingly, consciously; otherwise we use it blindly—use it we must.

In our growth from primitive man to conscious man, there are three seeming divisions or sections. First, our growth through the savage or unconscious state; second, our growth through the intellectual and conscious growing state; and third, our growth into, and conscious recognition of, our conscious state.

We all know that the bulb must first send out roots before it can send out shoots, and it must send out shoots before it can come to blossom in the sunlight. It is just so with us, like the plant, we must first send out roots (our roots are our thoughts), before we can evolve from our primitive or animal bulb-like state into the intellectual and conscious growing state.

Next we, like the plant, must send forth shoots before we can evolve from a purely intellectual state of conscious growing, into a conscious state of conscious knowing; otherwise we would always remain only creatures of the law and never masters of the law.

Lastly, we, like the plant, must individualize, must come to full blossom; in other words, must give forth the radiating beauty of a perfected life, must stand revealed to ourselves and to others, as a unit of power and a master over those laws that govern and control our growth. Each has a force within itself, and this force is the action of law set into activity by ourselves; it is through this consciousness that we begin to master laws, and to bring results through our conscious knowledge of their operation.

Life is a rigid conformity to laws, where we are the conscious or unconscious chemists of our own life; for when life is truly understood it is found to be made up of chemical action. As we breathe in oxygen, chemical action takes place in our blood; as we consume food and water, chemical action takes place in our digestive organs; in our use of thought chemical action takes place in both mind and body; in the change called death, chemical action takes place and disintegration sets in; so we find that physical existence is chemical action.

Life is made up of laws and as we make use of these laws, so do we get results.

If we think distress we get distress; if we think success, we get success. When we entertain destructive thought we set up a chemical action that checks digestion, which in turn irritates other organs of the body and reacts upon the mind, causing disease and sickness; when we worry, we churn a cess-pool of chemical action, causing fearful havoc to both mind and body; on the other hand, if we entertain constructive thoughts, we set up a healthy chemical action.

When we entertain negative thoughts, we put into action a poisonous chemical activity of a disintegrating nature, that stupefies our sensibilities and deadens our nerve actions, causing the mind and body to become negative and therefore subject to many ills; on the other hand, if we are positive, we put into action a healthy chemical activity of a constructive nature, causing the mind and body to become free from the many ills due to discordant thoughts.

These analyses can be carried through every avenue of life, but enough has been shown to indicate that life is largely chemical action, and that the mind is the chemical laboratory of thought, and that we are the chemists in the workshop of mental action where everything is prepared for our use, and where the product turned out will be in proportion to the material used; in other words, the nature of the thought we use determines the kind of conditions and experiences with which we meet; what we put into life we get out of life—no more, no less.

Life is an orderly advancement, governed by the "Law of Attraction." Our growth is through three seeming sections. In the first we are creatures of law, in the second users of law, and in the third we are masters of law. In the first we are unconscious users of thought power, in the second conscious users of thought power, and in the third we are conscious users of

conscious power. So long as we persist in
using only the laws of the first section we
are held in bondage to them; so long as we
remain satisfied with the laws and growth
of the second section we shall never become conscious of a greater advancement.
In the third section we awaken to our conscious power over laws of the first and second sections, and become fully awake to
the laws governing the third.

When rightly understood, life is found
not to be a question of chance; not a question of creed; not a question of nationality;
not a question of social standing; not a
question of wealth; not a question of power, NO—all of these have a place to fill in
the growth of the individual, but we must
all eventually come to know that Harmony
comes only as the result of a compliance
with Natural Law.

This rigid exactness and stability in the
nature of law is our greatest asset, and
when we become conscious of this available
power, and use it judiciously, we shall have
found the Truth which will make us Free!

Science has of late made such vast discoveries, has revealed such an infinity of resources, has unveiled such enormous possibilities and such unsuspected forces, that scientific men more and more hesitate to affirm certain theories as established and indubitable, or to deny certain other theories as absurd or impossible; and so a new civilization is being born; customs, creeds and cruelty are passing; vision, faith and service are taking their place. The fetters of tradition are being melted off from humanity, and as the dross of militarism and materialism are being consumed, thought is being liberated and truth is rising full orbed before an astonished multitude.

"We have caught only a glimpse of the possibility of the rule of mind which means the rule of spirit. We have just begun to realize in a small degree what this newly discovered power may do for us. That it can bring success in this world's affairs is beginning to be understood and practiced by thousands."

"The whole world is on the eve of a new consciousness, a new power and a new realization of resources within the self. The last century saw the most magnificent material progress in history. May the new century produce the greatest progress in mental and spiritual power."

"Thought is deeper than all speech,
    Feeling deeper than all thought,
Soul to soul can never teach
    What unto itself is taught."

VIBRATION

Before any environment, harmonious or otherwise, can be created, action of some kind is necessary, and before any action is possible, there must be thought of some kind, either conscious or unconscious, and as thought is a product of mind, it becomes evident that Mind is the creative center from which all activities proceed.

It is not expected that any of the inherent laws which govern the modern business world as it is at present constituted can be suspended or repealed by any force on the same plane, but it is axiomatic 'that a higher law may overcome a lower one. Tree life causes the sap to ascend, not by repealing the law of gravity, but by surmounting it.

The naturalist who spends much of his time in observing visible phenomena is constantly creating power in that portion of his brain set apart for observation. The

result is that he becomes very much more
expert and skillful in knowing what he
sees, and grasping an infinite number of
details at a glance, than does his unobserv-
ing friend. He has reached this facility
by exercise of his brain. He deliberately
chose to enlarge his brain power in the line
of observation, so he deliberately exercised
that special faculty, over and over, with
increasing attention and concentration.
Now we have the result—a man learned in
the lore of observation far above his fellow.
Or, on he other hand, one can by stolid inaction, allow the delicate brain matter to
harden and ossify until his whole life is
barren and fruitless.

Every thought tends to become a material thing. Our desires are seed thoughts
that have a tendency to sprout and grow
and blossom and bear fruit. We are sowing these seeds every day. What shall the
harvest be? Each of us today is the result
of his past thinking. Later we shall be
the result of what we are now thinking. We
create our own character, personality and

environment by the thought which we originate, or entertain. Thought seeks its own. The law of mental attraction is an exact parallel to the law of atomic affinity. Mental currents are as real as electric, magnetic or heat currents. We attract the currents with which we are in harmony.

Lines of least resistance are formed by the constant action of the mind. The activity of the brain reacts upon the particular faculty of the brain employed. The latent power of the mind is developed by constant exercise. Each form of its activity becomes more perfect by practice. Exercises for the development of the mind present a variety of motives for consideration. They involve the development of the perceptive faculties, the cultivation of the emotions, the quickening of the imagination, the symmetrical unfoldment of the intuitive faculty, which without being able to give a reason frequently impels or prohibits choice, and finally the power of mind may be cultivated by the development of the moral character.

"The greatest man," said Seneca, "is he who chooses right with invincible determination." The greatest power of mind, then, depends upon its exercise in moral channels, and therefore requires that every conscious mental effort should involve a moral end. A developed moral consciousness modifies consideration of motives, and increases the force and continuity of action; consequently the well developed symmetrical character necessitates good physical, mental and moral health, and this combination creates initiative, power, resistless force, and necessarily success.

It will be found that Nature is constantly seeking to express Harmony in all things, is forever trying to bring about an harmonious adjustment, for every discord, every wound, every difficulty; therefore when thought is harmonious, Nature begins to create the material conditions, the possession of which are necessary in order to make up an harmonious environment.

When we understand that mind is the great creative power, what does not become possible? With Desire as the great creative energy, can we not see why Desire should be cultivated, controlled and directed in our lives and destinies? Men and women of strong mentality who dominate those around them, and often those far removed from them, really emanate currents charged with power which, coming in contact with the minds of others, cause the desires of the latter to be in accord with the mind of the strong individuality. Great masters of men possess this power to a marked degree. Their influence is felt far and near, and they secure compliance with their wishes by making others "want" to act in accord with them. In this way men of strong Desire and Imagination may and do exert powerful influence over the minds of others, leading the latter in the way desired.

No man is ever created without the inherent power in himself to help himself. The personality that understands its own intellectual and moral power of conquest will assert itself. It is this truth which an enfamined world craves today. The possibility of asserting a slumbering intellectual courage that clearly discerns, and a moral courage that grandly undertakes is open to all. There is a divine potency in every human being.

We speak of the sun as "rising" and "setting," though we know that this is simply an appearance of motion. To our senses the earth is apparently standing still, and yet we know it is revolving rapidly. We speak of a bell as a "sounding body," yet we know that all that the bell can do is to produce vibrations in the air. When these vibrations come at the rate of sixteen a second they cause a sound to be heard in the mind. It is possible for the mind to hear vibrations up to the rate of 38,000 a second. When the number increases beyond this all is silence again; so that we know that the sound is not in the bell; it is in our own mind.

We speak and even think of the sun as "giving light," yet we know it is simply giving forth energy which produces vibrations in the ether at the rate of four hundred trillion a second, causing what are termed light waves, so that we know that what we call light is simply a mode of motion, and the only light existent, is the sensation caused in the mind by the motion of these waves. When the number of vibrations increases, the light changes in color, each change in color being caused by shorter and more rapid vibrations; so that although we speak of the rose as being red, the grass as being green, or the sky as being blue, we know that these colors exist only in our minds, and are the sensations experienced by us as the result of the vibrations of light. When the vibrations are reduced below four hundred trillion a second, they no longer affect us as light, but we experience the sensation of heat.

So we have come to know that appearances exist for us only in our consciousness. Even time and space become annihilated, time being but the experience of succession, there being no past or future except as a thought relation to the present.

In the last analysis, therefore, we know that one principle governs and controls all existence. Every atom is forever conserved; whatever is parted with must inevitably be received somewhere. It cannot perish and it exists only for use. It can go only where it is attracted, and therefore required. We can receive only what we give, and we may give only to those who can receive; and it remains with us to determine our rate of growth and the degree of harmony that we shall express.

The laws under which we live are designed solely for our advantage. These laws are immutable and we cannot escape from their operation. All the great eternal forces act in solemn silence, but it is within our power to place ourselves in harmony with them and thus express a life of comparative peace and happiness.

Difficulties, inharmonies, obstacles, indicate that we are either refusing to give out what we no longer need, or refusing to accept what we require. Growth is attained through an exchange of the old for the new, of the good for the better; it is a conditional or reciprocal action, for each of us is a complete thought entity and the completeness makes it possible for us to receive only as we give. We cannot obtain what we lack if we tenaciously cling to what we have.

The Principle of Attraction operates to bring to us only what may be to our advantage. We are able to consciously control our conditions as we come to sense the purpose of what we attract, and are able to extract from each experience only what we require for our further growth. Our ability to do this determines the degree of harmony or happiness we attain.

The ability to appropriate what we require for our growth continually increases as we reach higher planes and broader visions, and the greater our ability to know what we require, the more certain we shall be to discern its presence, to attract it and to absorb it. Nothing may reach us except what is necesary for our growth. All conditions and experiences that come to us do so for our benefit. Difficulties and obstacles will continue to come until we absorb their wisdom and gather from them the essentials of further growth. That we reap what we sow, is mathematically exact. We gain permanent strength exactly to the extent of the effort required to overcome our difficulties.

The inexorable requirements of growth demand that we exert the greatest degree of attraction for what is perfectly in accord with us. Our highest happiness will be best attained through our understanding of and conscious co-operation with natural laws.

Our mind forces are often bound by the paralyzing suggestions that come to us from the crude thinking of the race, and which are accepted and acted upon without question. Impressions of fear, of worry, of disability and of inferiority are given us daily. These are sufficient reasons in themselves why men achieve so little—why the lives of multitudes are so barren of results, while all the time there are possibilities within them which need only the liberating touch of appreciation and wholesome ambition to expand into real greatness.

Women, perhaps even more than men, have been subject to these conditions. This is true because of their finer susceptibilities, making them more open to thought-vibrations from other minds, and because the flood of negative and repressive thoughts has been aimed more especially at them.

But it is being overcome. Florence Nightingale overcame it when she rose in the Crimea to heights of tender sympathy and executive ability previously unknown among women. Clara Barton, the head of the Red Cross, overcame it when she wrought a similar work in the armies of the Union. Jenny Lind overcame it when she showed her ability to command enormous financial rewards while at the same time gratifying the passionate desire of her nature and reaching the front rank of her day in musical art. And there is a long list of women singers, philanthropists,

writers and actresses who have proved
themselves capable of reaching the greatest literary, dramatic, artistic and socio-
logical achievement.

Women as well as men are beginning to
do their own thinking. They have awak-
ened to some conception of their possibilities. They demand that if life holds any
secrets, these shall be disclosed. At no
previous time has the influence and potency of thought received such careful and
discriminating investigation. While a
few seers have grasped the great fact that
mind is the universal substance, the basis
of all things, never before has this vital
truth penetrated the more general consciousness. Many minds are now striving
to give this wonderful truth definite ut-
terance. Modern science has taught us
that light and sound are simply different
intensities of motion, and this has led to
discoveries of forces within man that could
not have been conceived of until this revelation was made.

A new century has dawned, and now, standing in its light man sees something of the vastness of the meaning of life—something of its grandeur. Within that life is the germ of infinite potencies. One feels convinced that man's possibility of attainment cannot be measured, that boundary lines to his onward march are unthinkable. Standing on this height he finds that he can draw new power to himself from the Infinite energy of which he is a part.

Some men seem to attract success, power, wealth, attainment, with very little conscious effort; others conquer with great difficulty; still others fail altogether to reach their ambitions, desires and ideals. Why is this so? Why should some men realize their ambitions easily, others with difficulty, and still others not at all? The cause cannot be physical, else the most perfect men physically would be the most successful. The difference, therefore, must be mental—must be in the mind; hence mind must be the creative force, must constitute the sole difference between men. It is mind, therefore. which overcomes environment and every other obstacle in the path of man.

When the creative power of thought is fully understood, its effect will seem to be marvelous. But such results cannot be secured without proper application, diligence and concentration. The laws governing in the mental and spiritual world are as fixed and infallible as in the material world. To secure the desired results, then, it is necesary to know the law and to comply with it. A proper compliance with the law will be found to produce the desired result with invariable exactitude.

Scientists tell us that we live in the universal ether. This is formless, of itself, but it is pliable, and forms about us, in us and around us, according to our thought and word. We set it into activity by that which we think. Then that which manifests to us objectively is that which we have thought or said.

Thought is governed by law. The reason we have not manifested more faith is because of lack of understanding. We have not understood that everything works in exact accordance with definite law. The law of thought is as definite as the law of mathematics, or the law of electricity, or the law of gravitation. When we begin to understand that happiness, health, success, prosperity and every other condition or environment are results, and that these results are created by thinking, either consciously or unconsciously, we shall realize the importance of a working knowledge of the laws governing thought.

Those coming into a conscious realization of the power of thought find themselves in possession of the best that life can give; substantial things of a higher order become theirs, and these sublime realities are so constituted that they can be made tangible parts of daily personal life. They realize a world of higher power, and keep that power constantly working. This power is inexhaustible, limitless, and they are therefore carried forward from victory to victory. Obstacles that seem insurmountable are overcome. Enemies are changed to friends, conditions are overcome, elements transformed, fate is conquered.

The supply is inexhaustible, and the demand can be made along whatever lines we may desire. This is the mental law of demand and supply.

Our circumstances and environment are formed by our thoughts. We have, perhaps, been creating these conditions unconsciously. If they are unsatisfactory the remedy is to consciously alter our mental attitude and see our circumstances adjust themselves to the new mental condition. There is nothing strange or supernatural about this; it is simply the Law of Being. The thoughts which take root in the mind will certainly produce fruit after their kind. The greatest schemer cannot ''gather grapes of thorns, or figs of thistles.'' To improve our conditions we must first improve ourselves. Our thoughts and desires will be the first to show improvement.

To be in ignorance of the laws of Vibration is to be like a child playing with fire, or a man manipulating powerful chemicals without a knowledge of their nature and relations. This is universally true because Mind is the one great cause which produces all conditions in the lives of men and women.

Of course, mind creates negative conditions just as readily as favorable conditions, and when we consciously or unconsciously visualize every kind of lack, limitation and discord, we create these conditions; this is what many are unconsciously doing all the time.

This law as well as every other law is no respecter of persons, but is in constant operation and is relentlessly bringing to each individual exactly what he has created; in other words, "Whatsoever a man soweth, that shall he also reap."

Arthur Brisbane says, "Thought and its work include all the achievements of man."

Compare spirit and thought to the genius of the musician and the sound which issues from the musical instrument.

What the instrument is to the musician the brain of the man is to the spirit that inspires thought.

However great the musician, the genius must depend for its expression upon the instrument which gives it reality in the physical world, through sound waves produced in the material atmosphere, striking nerves that carry music to the brain.

Give Paderewski a piano out of tune and he can give you only discord and lack of harmony. Or give to Paganini, the greatest violinist that ever lived, a violin out of tune, and in spite of the genius of the musician you will hear only hideous, disagreeable sounds. The spirit of music must have the right instruments for its expression.

The spirit that inspires thought, the spirit of man, must have the right brain for its expression.

The more complicated and highly developed the instrument, the more displeasing to the ear is the result when the instrument is out of tune.

Among human beings a highly developed brain out of tune—for instance, the insane ravings of a powerful genius like Nietzche, with his mind broken down—is infinitely more painful and shocking than in the case of a human being with a mind in comparison feeble and simple.

Our minds are so little accustomed to deal with the abstract, we live so much in the material world, inanimate objects have so much meaning for us that many human beings live and die without ever thinking at all of the spirit, yet the spirit is the only real thing in the universe.

And thought is the expression of spirit, working through a more or less imperfect human brain.

Bring yourself to think for some time earnestly of the nature and mysterious power of spirit. There is no thought more inspiring, fascinating, bewildering.

Consider the Falls of Niagara, with their tremendous power, the vast moving machinery, the cities that are lighted, the blazing streets, the moving cars, all due apparently to the power in Niagara. Yet not due to that power in reality so much as to the spirit expressed in the thought of man. It was spirit that harnessed Niagara. It was spirit transferred the power of the Falls to distant cities.

Yet that spirit has neither shape nor weight, size nor color, taste nor smell. You ask a man "What is the Spirit?" and he must answer that it is nothing, since it occupies no space, and cannot be seen or felt. And yet he must answer also that the spirit is everything. The world only exists as it is because we see it in the eyes of the spirit. The optic nerve takes a picture, sends it to the brain and the spirit sees the picture.

It was the spirit acting on the brain of Columbus, and through him upon others, that brought the first ship to America.

It is the spirit working and expressing itself through the thought of brains more and more highly developed that has gradually brought man from his former condition of savagery to his present comparative degree of civilization. And that same spirit, working in future ages through brains infinitely superior to any that we can now conceive, will establish real harmony on this planet.

Yet you know that spirit exists, and that it is you, and that except for that spirit which animates you, picks you up when you fall, inspires you in success and comforts you in failure and misfortune, there would be nothing at all in this life, and you would not be different from one of the stones in the field, or some of the dummies that the tailor sets in front of his store.

Compare the spirit and the material world as you see it with the genius that dwells in the brain of the great painter and the works which the painter has to do.

Every statue, painting and church that Michael Angelo created already existed in his spirit. But the spirit could not be content with that existence It had to visualize itself; it had to see itself created.

The spirit really lives completely only when it sees itself reflected in the material world. All the mother love is in the spirit of woman. But it has complete existence only when the mother holds the child in her arms and sees in reality, in flesh and blood, the being that she loves and has created.

The achievements of the greatest men are all locked up within them from the first, but the spirit of such men can reach full realization only when the spirit, acting through the brain and expressing itself through thought, creates the work.

We know that all useful work is the result of sound thought. If we realize that thought itself is the expression of the spirit, we are moved by a sense of duty to give to that spirit the best possible expression of which we are capable, the best chance that it can have, dwelling in imperfect bodies and speaking through imperfect minds such as those we possess.

It is an inspiration to realize that men here on earth, gradually improving, become less animal and more spiritual as the centuries pass, are destined to develop in their own physical bodies, instruments capable of interpreting properly the spirit that animates us.

Human beings improve from generation to generation—that we know. The improvement is due to the affection of fathers and mothers for each other and for their children.

This race of ours one hundred thousand years ago was made up of animal-like creatures, with huge, projecting jaws, enormous teeth, small foreheads and hideously shaped bodies. Gradually through the centuries we have changed, the brute has gradually disappeared, the prognathous face of man has become fatter. The jaw has gone in, the forehead has come out, and behind the forehead, gradually, thanks to the devotion and patient labor of women, we are developing a brain that will ultimately give decent and adequate expression to spirit.

Spirit and thought are identical in the sense that the genius of the musician and the sound that you hear when his music is played are identical. In music the sound represents and interprets the musician's spirit. And the interpretation and the accuracy of that interpretation depend upon the orchestra, the violin or the piano. When the instruments are out of tune it is not the genius of the musician, but a misinterpretation that you hear.

And with our human brains, most of them out of tune, most of them incapable of expressing anything but the merest, faintest reflection of true spiritual life, there is as yet very little harmony.

Through the perfected brain of man, the cosmic spirit, in which each of us is a conscious atom, will speak clearly, and then this earth, our little corner in the universe, will be truly harmonious, governed by the spirit distinctly expressed and instantly obeyed.

This cosmic spirit can and frequently does, operate through the brain of another. Many a man seems to be doing something very wonderful when in reality another man—another mind, not visible in the work, but actually at the work—does the heavy pulling.

You may see the salesman, the editor, the floor walker, the engineer, the architect —any kind of a man engaged in any kind of work—apparently doing something wonderful.

Yet he is not doing it all. An unseen power—another man, another brain, perhaps some little man with a small body and a big head, who keeps out of sight— is doing the work.

Every one of us without exception is pulled along or pushed ahead by some force unseen. It may be the man in the inside office, usually invisible. It may be the woman at home setting a good example, giving to the man at work the inspiration and the power that no one else could give. It may be paternal affection, enabling a man to do for a child what he could not possibly do for himself.

Very often the power is one that has long disappeared from the earth, a father or a mother whose energy and inspiration persists and does in the life of the son at work what the man could never have accomplished of his own accord.''

Cause and effect is as absolute and undeviating in the hidden realm of thought as in the world of visible and material things. Mind is the master weaver, both of the inner garment of character and the outer garment of circumstance.

—James Allen.

TRANSMUTATION.

Abundance is a natural law of the universe. The evidence of this law is conclusive; we see it on every hand. Everywhere Nature is lavish, wasteful, extravagant. Nowhere is economy observed in any created thing. The millions and millions of trees and flowers and plants and animals and the vast scheme of reproduction where the process of creating and re-creating is forever going on, all indicate the lavishness with which nature has made provision for man. That there is an abundance for everyone is evident; but that many seem to have been separated from this supply is also evident; they have not yet come into realization of the universality of all substance and that mind is the active principle which starts causes in motion whereby we are related to the things we desire.

To control circumstances, a knowledge of
certain scientific principles of mind-action
is required. Such knowledge is a most
valuable asset. It may be gained by degrees and put into practice as fast as
learned. Power over circumstances is one
of its fruits; health, harmony and prosperity are assets upon its balance sheet
It costs only the labor of harvesting its
great resources.

All wealth is the offspring of power; possessions are of value only as they confer
power. Events are significant only as they
affect power; all things represent certain
forms and degrees of power.

The discovery of a reign of law by which
this power could be made available for all
human efforts marked an important epoch
in human progress. It is the dividing line
between superstition and intelligence; it
eliminated the element of caprice in men's
lives and substituted absolute, immutable
universal law.

A knowledge of cause and effect as
shown by the laws governing steam, elec-

tricity, chemical affinity and gravitation enables men to plan courageously and to execute fearlessly. These laws are called Natural Laws, because they govern the physical world, but all power is not physical power; there is also mental power, and there is moral and spiritual power.

Thought is the vital force or energy which is being developed and which has produced such startling results in the last half century, as to bring about a world which would be absolutely inconceivable to a man existing only 50 or even 25 years ago. If such results have been secured by organizing these mental powerhouses in 50 years, what may not be expected in another 50 years?

Some will say, if these principles are true, why are we not demonstrating them; as the fundamental principle is obviously correct, why do we not get proper results? We do; we get results in exact accordance with our understanding of the law and our ability to make the proper application. We did not secure results from the laws gov-

erning electricity until someone formulated
the law and showed us how to apply it.
Mental action inaugurates a series of vibrations in the ether, which is the substance from which all things proceed,
which in their turn induce a corresponding
grosser vibration in the molecular substance until finally mechanical action is
produced.

This puts us in an entirely new relation
to our environment, opening out possibilities hitherto undreamt of, and this by
an orderly sequence of law which is naturally involved in our new mental attitude.

It is clear, therefore, that thoughts of
abundance will respond only to similar
thoughts; the wealth of the individual is
seen to be what he inherently is. Affluence
within is found to be the secret of attraction for affluence without. The ability to
produce is found to be the real source of
wealth of the individual. It is for this
reason that he who has his heart in his
work is certain to meet with unbounded
success. He will give and continually give,
and the more he gives the more he will receive.

Thought is the energy by which the law of attraction is brought into operation, which eventually manifests in abundance in the lives of men.

The source of all power, as of all weakness, is from within; the secret of all success as well as all failure is likewise from within. All growth is an unfoldment from within. This is evident from all Nature; every plant, every animal, every human is a living testimony to this great law, and the error of the ages is in looking for strength or power from without.

A thorough understanding of this great law which permeates the Universe leads to the acquirement of that state of mind which develops and unfolds a creative thought which will produce magical changes in life. Golden opportunities will be strewn across your path, and the power and perception to properly utilize them will spring up within you, friends will come unbidden, circumstances will adjust themselves to changed conditions; you will have found the "Pearl of greatest price."

Wisdom, strength, courage and all harmonious conditions are the result of power, and we have seen that all power is from within; likewise every lack, limitation or adverse circumstance is the result of weakness, and weakness is simply absence of power; it comes from nowhere; it is nothing—the remedy, then is simply to develop power.

This is the key with which many are converting loss into gain, fear into courage, despair into joy, hope into fruition.

This may seem to be too good to be true, but remember that within a few years, by the touch of a button or the turn of a lever, science has placed almost infinite resources at the disposal of man Is it not possible that there are other laws containing still great possibilities?

Let us see what are the most powerful forces in Nature. In the mineral world everything is solid and fixed. In the animal and vegetable kingdom it is in a state of flux, forever changing, always being created and recreated. In the atmosphere we find heat, light and energy. Each realm becomes finer and more spiritual as we pass from the visible to the invisible, from the coarse to the fine, from the low potentiality to the high potentiality. When we reach the invisible we find energy in its purest and most volatile state.

And as the most powerful forces of Nature are the invisible forces, so we find that the most powerful forces of man are his invisible forces, his spiritual force, and the only way in which the spiritual force can manifest is through the process of thinking. Thinking is the only activity which the spirit possesses, and thought is the only product of thinking.

Addition and subtraction are therefore spiritual transactions; reasoning is a spiritual process; ideas are spiritual conceptions; questions are spiritual searchlights and logic, argument and philosophy are parts of the spiritual machinery.

Every thought brings into action certain physical tissue, parts of the brain, nerve or muscle. This produces an actual physical change in the construction of the tissue.

Therefore it is only necessary to have a certain number of thoughts on a given subject in order to bring about a complete change in the physical organization of a man.

This is the process by which failure is changed to success. Thoughts of courage, power, inspiration, harmony, are substituted for thoughts of failure, despair, lack, limitation and discord, and as these thoughts take root, the physical tissue is changed and the individual sees life in a new light, old things have actually passed away; all things have become new; he is born again, this time born of the spirit; life has a new meaning for him; he is reconstructed and is filled with joy, confidence, hope, energy. He sees opportunities for success to which he was heretofore blind. He recognizes possibilities which before had no meaning for him. The thoughts of success with which he has been impregnated are radiated to those around him, and they in turn help him onward and upward; he attracts to him new and suc-

cessful associates, and this in turn changes
his environment; so that by this simple exercise of thought, a man changes not only
himself, but his environment, circumstances and conditions.

You will see, you must see, that we are
at the dawn of a new day; that the possibilities are so wonderful, so fascinating, so
limitless as to be almost bewildering. A
century ago any man with an aeroplane or
even a Gatling gun could have annihilated
a whole army equipped with the imple-
ments of warfare then in use. So it is at
present. Any man with a knowledge of
the possibilities of modern metaphysics
has an inconceivable advantage over the
multitude.

Mind is creative and operates through
the law of attraction. We are not to try to
influence anyone to do what we think they
should do. Each individual has a right to
choose for himself, but aside from this we
would be operating under the laws of
force, which is destructive in its nature and
just the opposite of the law of attraction.

A little reflection will convince you that all the great laws of nature operate in silence and that the underlying principle is the law of attraction. It is only destructive processes, such as earthquakes and catastrophies, that employ force. Nothing good is ever accomplished in that way.

To be successful, attention must invariably be directed to the creative plane; it must never be competitive. You do not wish to take anything away from any one else; you want to create something for yourself, and what you want for yourself you are perfectly willing that every one else should have.

You know that it is not necessary to take from one to give to another, but that the supply for all is abundant. Nature's storehouse of wealth is inexhaustible and if there seems to be a lack of supply anywhere it is only because the channels of distribution are as yet imperfect.

Abundance depends upon a recognition of the laws of Abundance. Mind is not only the creator, but the only creator of

all there is. Certainly nothing can be
created before we know that it can be
created and then make the proper effort.
There is no more Electricity in the world
today than there was fifty years ago, but
until someone recognized the law by which
it could be made of service, we received no
benefit; now that the law is understood,
practically the whole world is illuminated
by it. So with the law of Abundance; it is
only those who recognize the law and place
themselves in harmony with it, who share
in its benefits.

A recognition of the law of abundance
develops certain mental and moral qualities, among which are Courage, Loyalty,
Tact, Sagacity, Individuality and Constructiveness. These are all moods of
thought, and as all thought is creative, they
manifest in objective conditions corresponding with the mental condition. This
is necessarily true because the ability of
the individual to think is his ability to act
upon the Universal Mind and bring it into
manifestation; it is the process whereby

the individual becomes a channel for the differentiation of the Universal. Every thought is a cause and every condition an effect.

This principle endows the individual with seemingly transcendental possibilities, among which is the mastery of conditions through the creation and recognition of opportunities. This creation of opportunity implies the existence or creation of the necesary qualities or talents which are thought forces and which result in a consciousness of power which future events cannot disturb. It is this organization of victory or success within the mind, this consciousness of power within, which constitutes the responsive harmonious action whereby we are related to the objects and purposes which we seek. This is the law of attraction in action; this law, being the common property of all, can be exercised by any one having sufficient knowledge of its operation.

Courage is the power of the mind which manifests in the love of mental conflict; it is a noble and lofty sentiment; it is equally fitted to command or obey; both require courage. It often has a tendency to conceal itself. There are men and women, too, who apparently exist only to do what is pleasing to others, but when the time comes and the latent will is revealed, we find under the velvet glove an iron hand, and no mistake about it. True courage is cool, calm, and collected, and is never foolhardy, quarrelsome, ill-natured or contentious.

Accumulation is the power to reserve and preserve a part of the supply which we are constantly receiving, so as to be in a position to take advantage of the larger opportunities which will come as soon as we are ready for them. Has it not been said, "To him that hath shall be given"? All succesful business men have this quality, well developed. James J. Hill, who recently died, leaving an estate of over fifty-two million dollars, said: "If you want to know whether you are destined to be a success or failure in life, you can easily find out. The test is simple and it is infallible: Are you able to save money? If not, drop out. You will lose. You may think not, but you will lose as sure as you live. The seed of success is not in you.'' This is very good so far as it goes, but any one who knows the biography of James J. Hill knows that he acquired his fifty million dollars by following the exact methods we have given. In the first place, he started with nothing; he had to use his imagination to idealize the vast railroad which he projected across the western prairies. He then had to come into a recognition of the law of abundance in order to provide the ways and means for materializing it; unless he had followed out this program he would never have had anything to save.

Accumulativeness acquires momentum; the more you accumulate the more you desire, and the more you desire the more you accumulate, so that it is but a short time until the action and reaction acquire a momentum that cannot be stopped. It must, however, never be confounded with selfishness, miserliness or penuriousness; they are perversions and will make any true progress impossible.

Constructiveness is the creative instinct of the mind. It will be readily seen that every successful business man must be able to plan, develop or construct. In the business world it is usually referred to as initiative. It is not enough to go along in the beaten path. New ideas must be developed, new ways of doing things. It manifests in building, designing, planning, inventing, discovering, improving. It is a most valuable quality and must be constantly encouraged and developed. Every individual possesses it in some degree, because he is a center of consciousness in that infinite and Eternal Energy from which all things proceed.

Water manifests on three planes, as ice, as water and as steam; it is all the same compound; the only difference is the temperature, but no one would try to drive an engine with ice; convert it into steam and it easily takes up the load. So with your energy; if you want it to act on the crea-

tive plane, you will have to begin by melt-
ing the ice with the fire of imagination, and
you will find the stronger the fire, and the
more ice you melt, the more powerful your
thought will become, and the easier it will
be for you to materialize your desire.

Sagacity is the ability to perceive and
co-operate with Natural Law. True Sagacity avoids trickery and deceit as it would
leprosy; it is the product of that deep
insight which enables one to penetrate
into the heart of things and understand
how to set causes in motion which will inevitably create successful conditions.

Tact is a very subtle and at the same
time a very important factor in business
success. It is very similar to intuition. To
possess tact one must have a fine feeling,
must instinctively know what to say or
what to do. In order to be tactful one
must possess Sympathy and Understanding, the understanding which is so rare, for
all men see and hear and feel, but how des-
perately few "understand." Tact enables
one to foresee what is about to happen and

calculate the result of actions. Tact enables us to feel when we are in the presence of physical, mental and moral cleanliness, for these are today invariably demanded as the price of success.

Loyalty is one of the strongest links which bind men of strength and character. It is one which can never be broken with impunity. The man who would lose his right hand rather than betray a friend will never lack friends. The man who will stand in silent guard, until death, if need be, beside the shrine of confidence or friendship of those who have allowed him to enter will find himself linked with a current of cosmic power which will attract desirable conditions only. It is inconceivable that such a person should ever meet with lack of any kind.

Individuality is the power to unfold our own latent possibilities, to be a law unto ourselves, to be interested in the race rather than the goal. Strong men care nothing for the flock of imitators who trot complacently behind them. They derive no satisfaction in the mere leading of large numbers, or the plaudits of the mob. This pleases only petty natures and inferior minds. Individuality glories more in the unfolding of the power within than in the servility of the weakling.

Individuality is a real power inherent in all and the development and consequent expression of this power enables one to assume the responsibility of directing his own footsteps rather than stampeding after some self-assertive bell-wether.

Inspiration is the art of imbibing, the art of self realization, the art of adjusting the individual mind to that of the Universal Mind, the art of attaching the proper mechanism to the source of all power, the art of differentiating the formless into form, the art of becoming a channel for the flow of Infinite Wisdom, the art of visualizing perfection, the art of realizing the Omnipresence of Omnipotence.

Truth is the imperative condition of all well being. To be sure, to know the truth and to stand confidently on it, is a satisfaction beside which no other is comparable. Truth is the underlying verity, the condition precedent to every successful business or social relation.

Every act not in harmony with Truth, whether through ignorance or design, cuts the ground from under our feet, leads to discord, inevitable loss, and confusion, for while the humblest mind can accurately foretell the result of every correct action, the greatest, most profound and penetrating mind loses its way hopelessly and can form no conception of the result due to a departure from correct principles.

Those who establish within themselves the requisite elements of true success have established confidence, organized victory, and it only remains for them to take such steps from time to time as the newly-awakened thought force will direct, and herein rests the magical secret of all power.

Less than 10 per cent of our mental processes are conscious; the other 90 per cent are subconscious and unconscious, so that he who would depend upon his conscious thought alone for results is less than 10 per cent efficient. Those who are accomplishing anything worth while are those who are enabled to take advantage of this greater storehouse of mental wealth. It is in the vast domain of the subconscious mind that great truths are hidden, and it is here that thought finds its creative power, its power to correlate with its object, to bring out of the unseen the seen.

Those familiar with the laws of Electricity understand the principle that electricity must always pass from a higher to a lower potentiality and can therefore make whatever application of the power they desire. Those not familiar with this law can effect nothing; and so with the law governing in the Mental World; those who understand that Mind penetrates all things, is Omnipresent and is responsive to every demand, can make use of the law and can control conditions, circumstances and environment; the uninformed cannot use it because they do not know it.

The fruit of this knowledge is as it were, a gift of the Gods; it is the "truth" that makes men free, not only free from every lack and limitation, but free from sorrow, worry and care, and, is it not wonderful to realize that this law is no respecter of persons, that it makes no difference what your habit of thought may be, the way has been prepared?

With the realization that this mental power controls and directs every other power which exists, that it can be cultivated and developed, that no limitation can be placed upon its activity, it will become apparent that it is the greatest fact in the world, the remedy for every ill, the solution for every difficulty, the gratification of every desire; in fact, that it is the Creator's magnificent provision for the emancipation of mankind.

THOUGHTS ARE THINGS.

(Henry Van Dyke.)

I hold it true that thoughts are things;
They're endowed with bodies and breath and wings;
And that we send them forth to fill
The world with good results, or ill.
That which we call our secret thought
Speeds forth to earth's remotest spot,
Leaving its blessings or its woes
Like tracks behind it as it goes.
We build our future, thought by thought,
For good or ill, yet know it not.
Yet, so the universe was wrought.
Thought is another name for fate;
Choose, then thy destiny and wait,
For love brings love and hate brings hate.

ATTAINMENT.

The nervous system is matter. Its energy is mind. It is therefore the instrument of the Universal Mind. It is the link between matter and spirit, between our consciousness and the Cosmic-Consciousness. It is the gateway of Infinite Power.

Both the Cerebro-spinal and the Sympathetic nervous systems are controlled by nervous energy that is alike in kind; and the two systems are so interwoven that their impulses can be sent from one to the other. Every activity of the body, every impulse of the nervous system, every thought, uses up nervous energy.

The system of nerves may be compared to a telegraph system; the nerve cells corresponding to the batteries, the fibres to the wires. In the batteries is generated electricity. The cells, however, do not generate nervous energy. They transform it and the fibres convey it. This energy is not a physical wave like electricity, light, or sound. It is MIND.

117

It bears the same relationship to the mind as a piano does to its player. The Mind can only have perfect expression when the instrument through which it functions is in order.

The organ of the Cerebro-spinal Nervous System is the Brain, the organ of the Sympathetic Nervous System is the Solar Plexus. The first is the voluntary or Conscious, the latter the involuntary or Subconscious.

It is through the Cerebro-spinal Nervous System and the Brain that we become conscious of possessions, hence all possession has its origin in consciousness. The undeveloped consciousness of a babe, or the inhibited consciousness of an idiot, cannot possess.

This mental condition—consciousness—increases in direct proportion to our acquisition of knowledge. Knowledge is acquired by observation, experience, and reflection. We become conscious of these possessions by the mind; so that we recognize that possession is based on consciousness; this consciousness we designate the world within. Those possessions of Form that we acquire are of the world without.

That which possesses in the world within is Mind. That which enables us to possess in the world without is also Mind. Mind manifests itself as thoughts, mental pictures, words, and actions. Thought is therefore Creative. Our power to use Thought to create the conditions, surroundings, and other experiences of life, depends upon our habit of thinking. What we do depends upon what we are; what we are is the result of what we habitually think. Before we can Do, we must BE; before we can BE we must control and direct the force of Thought within us.

Thought is Force. There are but two things in the universe; Force and Form. When we realize that we possess this Creative Power, and that we can control and direct it, and by it act on the forces and forms in the objective world, we shall have made our first experiment in Mental Chemistry.

The Universal Mind is the 'Substance' of all force and form, the Reality that underlies ALL. In accordance with fixed laws, from Itself, and by I^tself, is ALL brought into being and sustained. It is the Creative Power of Thought in its perfect expression. The Universal Mind is All Consciousness, All Power, and is Everywhere Present. It is essentially the same at every point of its presence, all mind is one mind. This explains the order and harmony of the universe. To apprehend this statement is to possess the ability to understand and solve every problem of life.

Mind has a two-fold expression—conscious or objective, and subconscious or subjective. We come into relationship with the world without by the objective mind; and with the world within by the subconscious mind. Though we are making a distinction between the conscious and the subconscious minds, such a distinction does not really exist; but this arrangement will be found convenient. All Mind is One

Mind; in all phases of the mental life there is an indivisible unity and oneness.

The sub-conscious mind connects us with the Universal Mind, and thus we are brought into direct relationship with all power. In the sub-consciousness is stored up the observations and experiences of life that have come to it through the conscious mind. It is the storehouse of memory. The sub-conscious mind is a great seed plot in which thoughts have been dropped, or experiences conveyed by observation, or happenings planted, to come up again into consciousness with the fruitage of their growth.

Consciousness is the inner, and Thought is the outward expression of power. The two are inseparable; it is impossible to be conscious of a thing without thinking of it.

We have captured the lightning and changed its name to electricity. We have harnessed the waters and made the remorseless flood our servant. By the miracle of thought we have quickened water into vapor to bear the burdens, and move the commerce of the world. We have called into being floating palaces that plough the highways of the deep. We have triumphed in our conquest of the air. Although we are moored in the silvern archepelago of the Milky Way, we have conquered time and space.

When two electric wires are in close proximity, the first carrying a heavier load of electricity than the second, the second will receive by induction some current from the first. This will illustrate the attitude of mankind to the Universal Mind. They are not consciously connected with the source of power.

If the second wire were attached to the first, it would become charged with as much electricity as it could carry. When we become conscious of Power, we become a 'live wire,' because by consciousness we are connected with the Power. In proportion to our ability to use power, we are enabled to meet the various situations which arise in life.

The Universal Mind is the source of all power and all form. We are channels through which this power is being manifested; consequently within us is power unlimited, possibilities without end, and all under the control of our own thought. Because we have these powers, because we are in living union with the Universal Mind, we may adjust or control every experience which may come to us.

There are no limitations to the Universal Mind, therefore the better we realize our oneness with this mind, the less conscious will we be of any limitation or lack, and the more conscious of power.

The Universal Mind is the same at every point of its presence, whether in the infinitely large or the infinitely small. The difference in the power relatively manifested lies entirely in the ability of expression. A stick of clay and a stick of dynamite of equal weight contain much the same amount of energy. But in the one it is readily set free, whereas in the other we have not yet learned how to release it.

In order to express we must create the corresponding condition in our consciousness. Either in the Silence or by repetition we impress this condition upon the subconsciousness.

Consciousness apprehends, and Thought manifests the conditions desired. Conditions in our life and in our environment are but the reflection of our predominant thoughts. So the importance of correct thinking cannot be over-estimated. "Having eyes and seeing not, having ears and hearing not, neither do they understand," is another way of expressing the truth that without consciousness there can be no apprehension.

Thought constructively used creates tendencies in the subconsciousness, these tendencies manifest themselves as character. The primary meaning of the word character is an engraved mark, as on a seal; and means: The peculiar qualities impressed by nature or habit on a person, which separates the person possessing them from all others. Character has an outward and an inward expression; the inward being Purpose, and the outward Ability.

Purpose directs the mind towards the ideal to be realized, the object to be accomplished, or the desire to be materialized. Purpose gives quality to thought. Ability is the capacity to co-operate with Omnipotence—although this may be done unconsciously. Our purpose and our ability determine our experiences in life. It is important that purpose and ability be balanced; when the former is greater than the latter 'the Dreamer' is produced; when ability is greater than purpose, impetuosity is the result, producing much useless activity.

By the law of attraction our experiences depend upon our mental attitude. Like is attracted to like. Mental attitude is as much the result of character as character is of mental attitude. Each acts and reacts on the other.

"Chance," "Fate," "Luck, and "Destiny" seem to be blind influences at work behind every experience. This is not so, but every experience is governed by immutable laws, which may be controlled so as to produce the conditions which we desire.

Everything visible and tangible in the universe is composed of matter, which is acted upon by force. As matter is known to us by its external appearances, we shall designate it as form.

Form may be divided into four classes: That possessing Form only or the in-organic, as for example, Iron, Marble, etc. Form that is living or the organic which has sensation and voluntary motion, as in Animals. Form that in addition is Conscious of its own being, and its possessions, as Man.

The fundamental principle underlying every successful business relation or social condition is the recognition of the difference between the world within and the world without, the subjective world and the objective world.

Around you, as the center of it, the world without revolves. Matter, organized life, people, thoughts, sounds, light and other vibrations, the universe itself with its numberless millions of phenomena; sending out vibrations toward you, vibrations of light, of sound, of touch; loudness, softness; of love, hate, of thoughts, good and bad, wise and unwise, true and untrue. These vibrations are directed toward you —your ego—by the smallest, as well as by the greatest, the farthest and the nearest. A few of them reach your world within, but the rest pass by, and as far as you are immediately concerned, are lost.

Some of these vibrations or forces are essential to your health, your power, your success, your happiness. How is it that they have passed you by, and have not been received in your world within?

When making a graphophone record, certain conditions must be observed. Everything coming within range of the transmitter will be recorded, provided that the disc to receive the vibrations has been properly prepared, and the requisite conditions are observed.

Assuming that the transmitter is perfect, any defect in the recording disc, will make a corresponding deficient record. For example: the disc may not be perfectly flat, or may not be moving at the correct speed, or the wax may be too soft, or too hard; or the contact of the needle may be imperfect.

The world within possesses sensibility, a faculty that catches the vibrations from the the world without, and conveys them to the world within. It is the link that joins the two worlds. This sensibility is a form of consciousness.

Considering consciousness as a general term, we may say that it is the result of the world without acting on the world within. This takes place continuously whether we are awake or asleep. Consciousness is the result of sensing or feeling.

We easily recognize three phases of consciousness, between each of which there are enormous differences.

1. Simple consciousness, which all animals possess in common. It is the sense of existence, by which we recognize that "we

are," and "that we are where we are;" and by which we perceive the various objects and varied scenes and conditions.

2. Self-consciousness, possessed by all mankind, except infants, and the mentally deficient. This gives us the power of self contemplation, i. e., the effect of the world without upon our world within. "Self contemplates self." Amongst many other results, language has thus come into existence, each word being a symbol for a thought or an idea.

3. Cosmic-consciousness, this form of consciousness is as much above self-consciousness as self-consciousness is above simple consciousness. It is as different from either as sight is different from hearing or touch. The blind can get no true notion of color, however keen his hearing or sensitive his touch.

Neither by simple consciousness nor by self-consciousness can one get any notion of cosmic-consciousness. It is not like either of them, any more than sight is like hearing. A deaf man can never learn of the value of music by means of his senses of sight or of touch.

Cosmic-consciousness is all forms of consciousness. It overrides time and space, for apart from the body and the world of matter, these do not exist.

The immutable law of consciousness is: that in the degree that the consciousness is developed, so is the development of power in the subjective, and its consequent manifestation in the objective.

Cosmic-consciousness is the result of the creation of the necessary conditions, so that the Universal Mind may function in the direction desired. All vibrations in harmony with the Ego's well being are caught and used.

When truth is directly apprehended, or becomes a part of consciousness, without the usual process of reasoning or observation, it is intuition. By intuition the mind instantly perceives the agreement or the disagreement between two ideas. The Ego always so recognizes truth.

By intuition the mind transforms knowledge into wisdom, experience into success, and takes into the world within the things that have been waiting for us in the world without. Intuition, then, is another phase of the Universal Mind that presents truth as facts of consciousness.

THE THINKER

Back of the beating hammer,
  By which the steel is wrought,
Back of the workshop's clamor,
  The seeker may find the Thought;
The thought that is ever master
  Of iron and steam and steel,
That rises above disaster
  And tramples it under heel!

—Berton Braley

PROMISE YOURSELF

To be so strong that nothing can disturb your peace of mind.

To talk health, happiness and prosperity to every person you meet.

To make all your friends feel that there is something in them.

To look on the sunny side of everything and make your optimism come true.

To think only of the best, to work only for the best, and to expect only the best.

To be just as enthusiastic about success of others as you are about your own.

To forget the mistakes of the past and press on to the greater achievements of the future.

To wear a cheerful countenance at all times and to have a smile ready for every living creature you meet.

To give so much time to the improvement of yourself that you have no time to criticise others.

To be too large for worry, too noble for anger, too strong for fear, and too happy to permit the presence of trouble.

To think well of yourself and to proclaim this fact to the world—not in loud words, but in great deeds.

To live in the faith that the world is on your side so long as you are true to the best that is in you.

—Christen D. Larson.

INDUSTRY.

All the lost mines of Mexico, all the argosies that ever sailed from the Indies, all the gold and silver-laden ships of the treasure fleets of storied Spain, count no more in value than a beggar's dole compared to the wealth that is created every eight hours by modern business ideas.

Opportunity follows perception, action follows inspiration, growth follows knowledge, environment follows progress, always the mental first, then the transformation into the illimitable possibilities of character and achievement.

The progress of the United States is due to two per cent of its population. In other words, all our railroads, all our telephones, our automobiles, our libraries, our newspapers, and a thousand other conveniences, comforts and necessities are due to the creative genius of two per cent of the population.

133

As a natural consequence, the same two per cent are the millionaires of our country. Now, who are these millionaires, these creative geniuses, these men of ability and energy, to whom we owe practically all the benefits of civilization? The same authority tells us that thirty per cent of them are the sons of poor preachers who had never earned more than $1,500 a year; twenty-five per cent were the sons of teachers, doctors, and country lawyers; and only five per cent were the sons of bankers.

We are interested, therefore, in ascertaining why the two per cent succeeded in acquiring all that is best in life, and the ninety-eight per cent remain in perpetual want. We know that this is not a matter of chance, because the universe as we know it, is governed by law. Law governs solar systems, sun, stars, planets. Law governs every form of light, heat, sound, and energy. Law governs every material thing and every immaterial thought. Law covers the earth with beauty and fills it with bounty—shall we then not be certain that it also governs the distribution of this bounty?

Financial affairs are governed by law just as surely, just as positively, just as definitely, as health, growth, harmony, or any other condition in life, and the law is one with which anyone can comply.

Many are already unconsciously complying with this law; others are consciously coming into harmony with it.

Compliance with the law means joining the ranks of the two per cent; in fact, the new era, the golden age, the industrial emancipation, means that the two per cent is about to expand until the prevailing conditions shall have been reversed—the two per cent will soon become the ninety-eight per cent.

In seeking the truth we are seeking ultimate cause; we know that every human experience is an effect; therefore, if we may ascertain the cause, and if we shall find that this cause is one which we can consciously control, the effect or the experience will be within our control also.

Human experience will then no longer be the football of fate; a man will not be the child of fortune; but destiny, fate and fortune will be controlled as readily as a captain controls his vessel, or an engineer his train.

All things are finally resolvable into the same element, and as they are thus translatable, one into the other, they must ever be in relation and may never be in opposition to one another.

In the physical world there are innumerable contrasts, and these may, for the sake of convenience, be designated by distinctive names. There are surfaces, colors, shades, dimensions, or ends to all things. There is a North Pole, and a South Pole; an inside and an outside; a seen and an unseen; but these expressions merely serve to place extremes in contrast.

They are names given to two different parts or aspects of the same quantity. The two extremes are relative; they are not separate entities, but are two parts or aspects of one whole.

In the mental world we find the same law. We speak of knowledge and ignorance, but ignorance is but a lack of knowledge and is therefore found to be simply a word to express the absence of knowledge; it has no principle in itself.

In the moral world we speak of good and evil, but upon investigation, we find that good and evil are but relative terms. Thought precedes and predetermines action; if this action results in benefit to ourselves and others, we call this result good. If this result is to the disadvantage of ourselves and others, we call it evil. Good and evil are therefore found to be simply words which have been coined to indicate the result of our actions, which in turn are the result of our thoughts.

In the Industrial World, we speak of Labor and Capital as if there were two separate and distinct classes, but Capital is wealth and wealth is a product of Labor, and Labor necessarily includes Industry of every kind—physical, mental, executive, and professional. Every man or woman who depends in whole or in part for his or her income upon the results of their effort in the Industrial World must be classed as Labor. We therefore find that in the Industrial World there is but one Principle and that is Labor, or Industry.

There are many who are seriously and earnestly trying to find the solution to the present industrial and social chaos, and we hear much of production, waste, efficiency —and sometimes something in regard to constructive thinking.

The thought that humanity is on the borderland of a new idea, that the dawn of a new era is at hand, that a new epoch in the history of the world is about to take place, is rapidly spreading from mind to mind, and is changing the preconceived ideas of man and his relation to Industry.

We know that every condition is the result of a cause, and that the same cause invariably produces the same result. What has been the cause of similar changes in the thought of the world; the Renaissance, the Reformation, the Industrial Revolution?

Always the discovery and discussion of new knowledge.

The elimination of competition by the centralization of industry into corporations and trusts, and the economies resulting therefrom, have set man to thinking.

He sees that competition is not necessary to progress and he is asking: ''What will be the outcome of the evolution which is taking place in the Industrial World?'' And gradually the thought begins to dawn, the thought which is rapidly germinating, which is about to burst forth in the minds of all men everywhere, the thought which is carrying men off their feet and crowding out every selfish idea, the thought that the emancipation of the Industrial World is at hand.

This is the thought which is arousing the enthusiasm of mankind as never before; this is the thought which is centralizing force and energy, and which will destroy every barrier between itself and its purpose. It is not a vision of the future; it is a vision of the present; it is at the door—and the door is open.

The creative instinct in the individual is his spiritual nature; it is a reflection of the Universal Creative Principle; it is therefore instinctive and innate; it cannot be eradicated; it can only be perverted.

Owing to the changes which have taken place in the Industrial World, this creative instinct no longer finds expression; a man cannot build his own house; he can no longer make his own garden; he can by no manner of means direct his own labor; he is therefore deprived of the greatest joy which can come to the individual, the joy of creating, of achievement; and so this great power for good is perverted and turned into destructive channels; becoming envious, he attempts to destroy the works of his more fortunate fellows.

Thought results in action. If we wish to change the nature of the action, we must change the thought, and the only way to change the thought is to substitute a healthy mental attitude for the chaotic mental conditions existing at present.

It is evident that the power of thought

is by far the greatest power in existence; it
is the power which controls every other
power, and while this knowledge has until
recently been the possession of the few,
it is about to become the priceless privilege of the many. Those who have the imagination, the vision, will see the opportunity of directing this thought into constructive and creative channels; they will
encourage and foster the spirit of mental
adventure; they will arouse, develop and
direct the creative instinct, in which case
we shall soon see such an industrial revival
as the world has never before experienced.

Henry Ford visions the approach of the
new Era in The Dearborn Independent. He
says:

"The human race is now on the border
line between two periods, the period when
to use is to lose, and the period when not
to use is to waste. For a long time mankind has been conscious of somehow coming to the end of irresponsible childhood;
the provision made by the Parent of mankind has seemed to be coming to the end of

its lavishness. That is, there has been a sense that the more we used the less we had in reserve. This feeling has been expressed in the popular adage, 'You can't eat your cake and have it.'

"But now that man is learning enough to plant his supply as well as reap it, to make his supply a recurrent crop instead of a slowly diminishing original store of natural resources, the time is coming when instead of being afraid of wasting our resources by using them we shall be afraid of wasting them by not using them. The stream of supply will be so full and constant that when people worry it will not be worry about not having enough, but about not using enough.

"If you can imagine a world in which the source of supply will be so plentiful that people will worry about not using enough of it, instead of worrying as we do now about using too much, you will have a picture of the world that is soon to be. We have long depended on the resources which nature long ago stored up, the resources which can be exhausted. We are entering an era when we shall create resources which shall be so constantly renewed that the only loss will be not to use them. There will be such a plenteous supply of heat, light and power, that it will be sin not to use all we want. This era is coming in now. And it is coming by way of Water.

"With the fuel question settled, and the light question settled, and the heating question settled, and the power question settled, on such terms as actually liberate the whole world from the crushing weight of these four great burdens; and not only that, but with the whole fuel and light and heat and power situation turned around so that people will have to use all that they want, in order to prevent waste —don't you see how economic life will swing loose and breathe deeply, as if a new spring day had dawned for humanity?

"That is the era we are approaching. There is no question about that. There will be, of course, the usual preliminary skirmish between selfishness and service, but service will win. The ownership of a coal mine located on a man's property may easily be granted to private parties but the ownership of a river! Nature itself rebukes the man who would claim ownership of a river.

"Our next period is before us, not the first period of reckless waste, nor the second period of anxious accounting, but the third period of overlapping abundance which compels us to use and use and use, to fulfill every need."

Thought is mind in motion, just as wind is air in motion. Mind is a spiritual activity; in fact, it is the only activity which the spiritual man possesses, and Spirit is the creative Principle of the Universe.

Therefore, when we think, we start a train of causation; the thoughts go forth and meet other similar thoughts; they coalesce and form ideas; the ideas now exist independently of the thinker; they are the invisible seeds which exist everywhere, and which sprout and grow and bring forth fruit, some an hundred—and some a thousandfold.

We have been led to believe, and many still seem to think, that Wealth is something very material and tangible; that we can secure and hold it for our own exclusive use and benefit. We somehow forget that all the gold in the world only amounts to a very few dollars per capita. The entire supply of gold for the world is only eight billion dollars.

This includes all the gold coined or in bars in the various banks or Government treasuries of the world. This quantity of gold could be easily contained in a sixty-foot cube. If we depended upon the supply of gold it would be exhausted in a single day, and yet with this as a basis we spend hundreds and thousands, millions and now billions, of dollars daily, and yet the original supply of gold is not altered. The gold is simply a measure, a rule; with one ruler we may measure thousands and hundreds of thousands of feet, so with one $5 bill hundreds and thousands and millions of people may have the use of it by simply passing it from one to the other.

So it is that if we can only keep the tokens of wealth, which we call money, circulating, everyone could have all he or she might want; there need be no lack. The sense of lack comes only when we begin to hoard, when we are seized with fear and panic and fail to give out, to release.

It is therefore evident that the only way we can get any benefit from wealth is by its use, and to use it we must give it out, so that someone else can get the benefit of it; we are then co-operating for our mutual benefit and putting the law of abundance into practical operation.

We also see that wealth is by no means as substantial and tangible as many suppose, but that, on the contrary, the only way to get it is to keep it going; as soon as there is any concerted movement whereby there is any danger of stopping the circulation of this médium of exchange there is stagnation, fever, panic, and industrial death.

It is this intangible nature of wealth that makes it peculiarly susceptible to the power of thought and has enabled many men to secure fortunes in a year or two which others could not hope to acquire in a lifetime of effort. This is due to the creative power of mind.

Helen Wilmans gives an interesting description of the practical operation of this law in "The Conquest of Poverty." She says:

"There is an almost universal reaching out for money. This reaching out is from the acquisitive faculties only, and its operations are confined to the competitive realm of the business world. It is a purely external proceeding; its mode of action is not rooted in the knowledge of the inner life, with its finer, more just, and spiritualized wants. It is but an extension of animality into the realm of the human, and no power can lift it to the divine plane the race is now approaching.

"For all lifting on this plane is the result of spiritual growth. It is doing just what Christ said we must do in order to be rich. It is first seeking the kingdom of heaven within, where alone it exists. After this kingdom is discovered, then all these things (external wealth) shall be added.

"What is there within a man that can be called the kingdom of heaven? When I answer this question not one reader out of ten will believe me—so utterly bankrupt of knowledge of their own internal wealth are the great majority of people. But I shall answer it, nevertheless, and it will be answered truly.

"Heaven exists within us in the faculties latent in the human brain, the superabundance of which no man has ever dreamed. The weakest man living has the powers of a God folded within his organization; and they will remain folded until he learns to believe in their existence, and then tries to develop them. Men generally are not introspective, and this is why they are not rich. They are poverty-stricken in their own opinions of themselves and their powers, and they put the stamp of their belief on everything they come in contact with. If a day laborer, let us say, does but

look within himself long enough to perceive that he has an intellect that can be
made as great and far reaching as that of
the man he serves; if he sees this, and at-
taches due importance to it, the mere fact
of his seeing it, has, to a degree, loosened
his bonds and brought him face to face
with better conditions.

"But there is wanted something more
than the fact of knowing that he is, or may
become, by recognition of self, his employer's intellectual equal. There remains the
fact that he needs also to know the Law
and claim its provisions; namely, that his
superior knowing relates him to a superior
position. He must know this and trust it;
for it is by holding this truth in faith and
trust that he begins to ascend bodily. Em-
ployers everywhere hail with delight the
acquisition of employes who are not mere
machines—they want brains in their business and are glad to pay for them. Cheap
help is often the most expensive, in the
sense of being the least profitable. As
brain growth or development of thought

power in the employe increases his value
to the employer, and as the employe grows
to the degree of strength where he is capable of doing for himself, there will be another not yet grown so strong to take his
place.

"The gradual recognition by a man of
his own latent powers is the heaven within that is to be brought forward in the
world and established in these conditions
which correlate it.

"A mental poor-house projects from itself the spirit of a visible poor-house, and
this spirit expresses itself in visible exter-
nals correlated to its character.

"A mental palace sends forth the spirit
of a visible palace with results that correlate it. And the same may be said of sickness and sin, of health and goodness."

ECONOMICS

Economics is the science which treats of the production and distribution of wealth, and of the means and methods of living well. The ancients felt that every piece of sculpture was the embodiment of an idea or sentiment, and was produced on the principle that there is a perfect correspondence between mental states and physical expression.

We of the present day recognize that there is a direct correspondence between mental states and the condition of the human body, and that knowledge has been so formulated that we now know that every condition is an effect, and this effect is a result of a cause which had its origin in an idea.

Modern science is now directing attention to the fact that ideas are also responsible for every form of wealth and its distribution. The science of economics is therefore seen to be the science which treats of the laws governing ideas and their expression on a material plane.

It takes the sun about two thousand years to pass from one sign of the Zodiac to another. In oriental literature these are called sub-race periods, for it is during such a period that a nation is born, matures, grows old and dies. Most of the European nations are now ending their two thousand year cycle, and the necessary readjustments are taking place. It remains then for us, a new nation, in a new world, to assist in the readjustment.

In this readjustment it might be well to remember that intelligence rules; that constructive thought, intelligently directed, automatically causes its object to materialize on the objective plane; that cause and effect are supreme in a universe governed by immutable law; that it is the mind alone which can furnish the knowledge with which to ameliorate the conditions of life. It is the mind which builds every house, writes every book, paints every picture; it is the mind which suffers and enjoys; it follows that a knowledge of the functions of the mind rank first in importance to the human race.

Senator Wadsworth recently said: "I pray that the time will come when American public opinion will come to an appreciation of what organic chemistry means, of what research means, in the way of progress. We have been interested as a people in the development of material resourcs—the digging of iron and coal from the ground, the raising of crops upon the surface, and the engaging in transportation and other forms of commercial effort. As a people we have paid little attention and given little encouragement to scientific research, but Mr. President and Senators, the progress of the future depends upon scientific research. It is the man working in the chemical laboratory who is to blaze the way for human progress."

He went on to say: "I believe that in organic chemistry lies the solution of the secrets of the past and of the future. I be-

lieve that its establishment and mainte-
nance in this country, even under an em-
bargo, means the happiness, the progress,
and the security of 100,000,000 people."

Senator Frelinghuysen added: "When
we realize that it was due to the genius of
the German chemists, and the advance in
the science by the German industries, that
enabled Germany to get almost to the channel ports; when we realize that the next
war will be fought with chemicals, I think
it is our patriotic duty to give this industry the highest protection that can be im-
posed."

It is true that many of the more important discoveries in science are due to the
genius of German chemists; it is also true
that the next war, if there be one, will be
fought with chemicals, but the next and
all future wars will be won by an understanding of mental chemistry.

Try to realize the situation, think for a
moment, see an army of men pass in review, four abreast, all men in the prime of

life, see them march on and on, men from
Germany, men from France, from England,
from Belgium, from Austria, from Russia,
from Poland, from Rumania, from Bulga-
ria, from Servia, from Turkey, yes and
from China and Japan, India, New Zea-
land, Australia, Egypt and America, on
they go, marching all day long, all the
next day and the day after, all the week
they keep coming and the next week, and
the next week, and the next month, for
if would take months for this army
of ten million men to pass any given
point. All dead, and dead only because a few men in high places were
more concerned about organic chemistry
than they were about mental chemistry.
They did not know that force can always
be met with equal or superior force; they
did not know that a higher law always controls a lower law, and because intelligent
men and women allowed a few men in high
places to control their thinking processes,
the entire world must sit in sack-cloth and
ashes, for the living will find it necessary

to work the rest of their lives in order to even pay the interest on the obligations assumed and their children will find these obligations an inheritance, and they in turn will pass them on to their children and their children's children.

A celebrated European statesman visions the present situation as follows:

"Unfortunately, the ills of a war like that of 1914-1918 are repaired but with difficulty. Given even the entire good faith of the conquered, if the latter by conscientious labor genuinely desired to help the world out of its sanguinary nightmare and back to normal life, that world would none the less remain for a long time hopelessly adrift and at sea. We are assisting today at the prolongation of a war which is not even likely to approach a conclusion unless there is a new orientation of a peace-time energy. Finances upside down, budgets artificially met, rates of exchange giving 65 francs to the pound and 14 to the dollar, a terribly distorted fiduciary circulation, an ever-increasing cost of living, strikes, rapid changes in the stock markets, making commerce and industry impossible; accumulation of stocks—such is the ransom of these four years of war. It was materially impossible that either for conqueror or conquered aught else should result from this world catastrophe than complete chaos for all. Millions of men are not consecrated for 52 months to a work of death and destruction for the world to be re-established on the morrow of peace. Such rapidity reacquired equilibrium is beyond the bounds of human practicability."

It will be remembered that the Master Metaphysician said the same thing in somewhat different language many years ago:

"Then shall be great tribulation such as never was since the beginning of the world, nor never shall be afterwards, and if that period would not be shortened no flesh at all would be saved, but for the elect's sake that period will be shortened."—Matt. 24:21, 22.

That people are beginning to think is evident; formerly when men were discontented or dissatisfied they met in a near-by saloon, had a few drinks and promptly forgot their discontent and dissatisfaction. The situation is very different under existing conditions, men spend their time reading, studying and thinking, and the more they think the less satisfied they become.

Leaders of men all know this, for this reason England has her ale, Scotland her whisky, France her absinthe, Germany her beer and we of America who are recruited from all of these have had all forms of alcohol, it is by far the easiest way of keeping the people ''happy and contented.'' A man who has access to a fair percentage of alcohol, will not ask too many questions, if he does give him another drink.

This method of reducing the citizens of a country to a kind of idiotic servility has the additional advantage in that it produces enormous revenues which may be used for reducing them to economic slavery as well as spiritual slavery, for the man who cannot think has but small prospect of ever coming into any understanding of spiritual truth.

But because the opium traffic furnishes millions of revenue for Englishmen, millions of Chinese must be sacrificed, and because the sale and distribution of alcohol furnishes million dollar accounts for large banks and trust companies, $100,000.00 fees for corporation attorneys, because it makes it possible to lead large masses of men to the polls for the purpose of voting for political parties which are both morally and politically bankrupt, there are those who would again inflict this deadly curse upon the citizens of our country.

Dr. Woods Hutchinson tells us that the death rate for the United States has fallen in the last three years from 14.2 to 12.3 a thousand, which represents a saving of over 200,000 lives a year since the brewers' business was closed down. "Almost unanimous reports from public school teachers, school and district nurses, welfare workers among the poor, intelligent police chiefs and heads of charitable organizations, show that never, in all their experience, has there been so striking an improvement in the feeding, the clothing, the general comfort and welfare of school children as within the last two years.''

And yet there are those who favor the modification of the Volstead act. There is probably not a single individual in existence whose thinking processes are in such an infantile stage of development that he does not know that when a door has been partly opened it requires but the pressure of the little finger to push it wide open, so that modification is but another word for annullment with all of its physical, mental, moral and spiritual degradation and disaster, and all of the sorrow, suffering, infamy, shame and horror which this most monstrous curse has inflicted upon suffering humanity.

Happiness, prosperity and contentment are the result of clear thinking and right action, for the thought precedes and predetermines the nature of the action. A little artificial stimulation in the form of intoxicating liquor may temporarily still the senses and thus serve to confuse the issue, but as in economics and mechanics every action is followed by a reaction, so in human relations every action is followed by an equal reaction, and so we have come to know that the value of things depends upon the recognition of the value of persons. Whenever a creed becomes current that things are of more importance than people programs become fixed which set the interest of wealth above the interests of people, this action must necessarily be followed by a reaction.

Experience has decided that any stimulus applied stately to the stomach, which raises its muscular tone above the point at which it can be sustained by food and sleep, produces, when it has passed away, debility —a relaxation of the overworked organ, proportioned to its preternatural excitement. The life-giving power of the stomach falls of course as much below the tone of cheerfulness and health, as it was injudiciously raised above it. **If the experiment** be repeated often, it produces an artificial tone of stomach, essential to cheerfulness and muscular vigor, entirely above the power of the regular sustenance of nature to sustain, and creates a vacuum which nothing can fill but the destructive power which made it; and when protracted use has made the difference great between the natural and this artificial tone, and habit has made it a second nature, the man is a drunkard, and in ninety-nine instances in a hundred is irretrievably undone.

Beer has been recommended as a substitute, and a means of leading back the captive to health and liberty. But though it may not create intemperate habits as soon, it has no power to allay them. It will even finish what alcohol has begun, and with this difference only, that it does not rasp the vital organs with quite so keen a file, and enables the victim to come down to his grave by a course somewhat more dilatory, and with more of the goodnatured stupidity of the idiot and less of the demoniac frenzy of the madman.

Wine has been prescribed as a means of decoying the intemperate from the ways of death. But habit cannot be thus cheated out of its dominion, nor ravening appetite be amused down to a sober and temperate demand. It is not true that wine will restore the intemperate, or stay the progress of the disease. Enough must be taken to screw up nature to the tone of cheerfulness, or she will cry, "Give," with an importunity not to be resisted; and long before the work of death is done, wine will fail to minister a stimulus of sufficient activity to rouse the flagging spirits, or will become acid on the enfeebled stomach, and whisky and brandy will be called in to hasten to its consummation the dilatory work of self-destruction.

The history of the world confirms this conclusion. Egypt, once at the head of nations, has, under the weight of her own effeminacy, gone down to the dust. The victories of Greece let in upon her the luxuries of the East, and covered her glory with a night of ages. And Rome, whose iron foot trod down the nations and shook the earth, witnessed in her latter days faintness of heart and the shield of the mighty vilely cast away.

Marion Leroy Burton, President of the University of Michigan, says: ''Perhaps the most solemn question that can be put to a person today is, 'Can you think?' The test of individual efficiency and usefulness to society centers in a man's ability to use his mind. Emerson never erected a more arresting danger signal than when he exclaimed: 'Beware when the great God lets loose a thinker on the planet.' If we could only harness the mental power of America today we could solve the gigantic problems of the world. Not by appeals to prejudice and class interest, not by the hurling of epithets, not by the ready acceptance of half truths, not by superficial, but by careful, painstaking, scientific, scholarly thought combined with wise and timely action, will civilization be rescued and human freedom made secure. Upon Education depends the future of Democracy. Therefore, every loyal citizen, every self-respecting person, must utilize his opportunities to strengthen his grip on knowledge and to stimulate his mind. The truth has always made men free, and truth is available only for him who thinks.''

Roger W. Babson says: ''If statistics have taught us any one thing during the past twenty years, it is that the spiritual factor is the greatest factor in the growth of communities and nations. It is well enough to talk about land, labor and capital. They all have their uses and functions, but of themselves they are helpless in bringing about prosperity. Land, labor and capital existed long before there was even civilization. Many great nations, such as Babylon, Persia, Egypt, Greece, Rome and even Spain, have possessed land, labor and capital in abundance, but fell for want of this far more important quality—the spiritual factor.

"I'm looking out of my window at the highway where a man is at work with a pick. The highway is the *land;* the man is the *labor;* and the pick is the *capital.* This is a perfect illustration of land, labor and capital; but it also illustrates that such a combination can be used either to destroy or to construct,—to break up the road, or to repair the road. The man can use the pick to make the ruts and holes deeper, or to fill them up. It all depends upon the purpose, the motive and the desire of the man. Purpose, motive and desire are spiritual factors and are all important. Land, labor and capital, and even education, are mere tools which can be used either for good or for evil. Two men graduate from the same law school and get the same degree;—one uses his education to *uphold* the law, and the other uses his education to help men *evade* the law. Two chemists graduate from the same technical school in the same class;—one uses his training to make foods *pure;* and the other uses the same training to *adulterate* foods."

Thinking is a creative process and combination is the key. Nature combines electrons, atoms, molecules, cells and the final result is the Universe. In the field of human endeavor all progression, development and achievement is the result of following the lesson learned from nature, and man has risen step by step from the primitive brute state to his present position of mastership by combining, uniting and relating thoughts, things and forces.

In the domain of science and invention, in the realm of art, literature, and business, in every department of human activity, by combining the common, the usual, the known, man has unveiled and discovered the uncommon, the unusual, the unknown. Man has progressed rapidly in spite of the fact that the method pursued in finding out new combinations was used unconsciously and unsystematically. In order to eliminate accident and chance, there must be employed a scientific method, applied consciously and systematically, exhaustively, earnestly, honestly, continuously, resulting in greater success, more wonderful discoveries, more numerous and astounding inventions.

Mental Chemistry is a scientific method of creating new ideas, of mastering any subject, of mastering and increasing any business, of mastering any profession, or of solving any problem. This method will be worth nothing unless it is applied. If the application is made honestly, earnestly and systematically it will bring great results.

The method stated in a nutshell is the systematic combining of concepts. Conception is the mental act of grasping the common qualities of many objects and uniting them into a single notion. This single notion is a concept.

Make an inventory of all the concepts in your particular business or in any departments of nature, or in any sphere of human activity.

Study the inter-relation of each one in the list with every other one in it.

Your table of concepts must be an exhaustive list of every known fact, item, implement, law and method connected with your department of thought and labor.

If you have any special problem to solve select those concepts in your list which more directly apply to the thing you seek, and see how you can combine those you have thus selected out of the entire list.

To illustrate: Combine concept one with concept two, that will give you an idea. Combine concept one with concept three, that will give you an idea. Combine concept one with concept four, that will give you an idea. And so run concept one down the entire list of selected concepts or until such point when the idea you seek is forthcoming, but if you finish concept one without result then take up concept two and combine it with one, with three and four and so on to the end. This process will give you another set of new ideas.

Then take concept three down the line to the end, then concept four and so on until you find the idea you are searching for, or in case you wish to make a veritable thesaurus of new ideas, until you have treated every concept in the list to a relation with every other concept in it, then combine your concepts in pairs, then in threes and fours. Your list of concepts and such use of it as given above is almost an exhaustless fountain of new ideas which by this process multiply in rapid geometrical ratio.

The use of this method will solve any problem that may confront you. It will bring you success no matter what your goal may be. It will be more easily and quickly reached in Science, in Art, in Literature it will crown you with achievement in business, it will reflect in increased profits, in your environment by happiness and contentment. It will place you always on the right path provided that you use it earnestly, honestly and continuously.

MEDICINE

WHERE TRUTH ABIDES

Truth is within ourselves; it takes no rise
From outward things, whate'er you may believe,
There is an inmost center in us all,
Where Truth abides in fullness; and around,
Wall upon wall, the gross flesh hems it in,
This perfect clear conception—which is Truth.
A baffling and preverting carnal mesh
Blinds it, and makes all error; and, to know
Rather consists in opening out a way
Whence the imprisoned splendor may escape,
Than in effecting entry for a light
Supposed to be without.

—Robert Browning.

MEDICINE

The attitude of the practitioners of medicine toward mental chemistry has always been most catholic. To quote from Dr. Osler: "The psychical method has always played an important, though largely unrecognized, part in therapeutics. It is from faith, which buoys up the spirits, sets the blood flowing more freely, and the nerves playing their parts without disturbance, that a large part of all cures arise. Despondency or lack of faith will often sink the stoutest constitution almost to death's door; faith will enable a bread pill or a spoonful of clear water to do almost miracles of healing, when the best medicines have been given over in despair. The basis of the entire profession of medicine is faith in the doctor and his drugs and his methods."

F. W. Clarke has fitly summed up the relation of modern chemistry to progressive medicine: "Medicine is indebted to chemistry for almost a new pharmacopœia, for not only have new medicines been created, but in place of old drugs, crude and bulky, the compact and more elegant active principles are now employed. Anæsthetics, such as ether, chloroform and nitrous oxide; hypnotics like chloral; the remedies derived from coal-tar; and alkaloids like quinine, morphine, and cocaine, are a few of the contributions with which chemistry has enriched medical practice. Even antiseptic surgery depends upon chemical preparations for its success." On the other hand, Dr. Osler admits that, "We have not as yet made as many additions to the stock of panaceas as we might. But chemistry has done vast service for us, and will probably do far more. Aside from the discovery of new substances like cocaine, it has given us the active principles of calculable strength and purity, in place of crude drugs of varying strength at best, and of varying purity and age, and there is no reason why we may not have new specifics as sure (and for as important diseases) as quinine."

Our problem would be more simple, and the doctors, with their wide knowledge and splendid service, would have solved the problem long ago, had it been a purely physical one; but unfortunately it is a mental problem long before it becomes a physical one; as we continue to exercise our capacity for response we shall find it necessary to treat our thoughts and emotions if we are to establish health upon a firm basis.

For instance, it is commonly recognized that worry or continued negative emotional excitement will disorganize digestion. When the digestion is normal the feeling of hunger will stop, will be inhibited when we have eaten as much as we need, nor will we feel hunger again until we actually require food. In such cases our inhibiting center is working properly. But if we get dyspeptic, this inhibiting center has ceased to function, and we are hungry all the time, with the consequent tendency to overwork an already impaired digestive apparatus. Mankind is continually experiencing such small disturbances. They are strictly local

and attract but small attention at the great
center. They come, and go—and properly
so—without drawing from the organism as
a whole much consideration. But if the
disorder has grown out of a deep-rooted
cause which cannot easily be removed, disease of a more serious nature will ensue.
Under such circumstances, by reason of its
seriousness and long continuance, the trouble involves all parts of the organism and
may threaten its very life. When it reaches
this point, if the administration at the
grand center is vigorous and determined
and wise, the disturbance cannot long en-
dure; but if there is weakness at that center the whole federation may go down with
a crash.

Dr. Lindlahr says that "Nature Cure
Philosophy presents a rational concept of
evil, its cause and purpose, namely: that it
is brought on by violation of Nature's laws,
that it is corrective in its purpose that it
can be overcome only by compliance with
the Law. There is no suffering, disease or
evil of any kind anywhere unless the
law has been transgressed somewhere by
someone."

These transgressions of the law may be due to ignorance, to indifference, or to wilfulness and viciousness. The effect will always be commensurate with the causes.

The science of natural living and healing shows clearly that what we call disease is primarily Nature's effort to eliminate morbid matter and to restore the normal functions of the body; that the processes of disease are just as orderly in their way as everything else in Nature; that we must not check or suppress them, but co-operate with them. Thus we con, slowly but laboriously, the all-important lesson that "obedience to the law" is the only means of prevention of disease, and the only cure.

The Fundamental Law of Cure, the Law of Action, and Reaction, and the Law of Crisis, as revealed by the Nature Cure Philosophy, impress upon us the truth that there is nothing accidental or arbitrary in the processes of health, disease and cures; that every changing condition is either in harmony or in discord with the laws of our being; that only by complete surrender and obedience to the law can we master the law, and attain and maintain perfect physical health.

In our study of the cause and character of disease we must endeavor to begin at the beginning, and that is LIFE itself; for the processes of health, disease and cure are manifestations of that which we call life and vitality.

There are two prevalent, but widely differing conceptions of the nature of life or vital force: the material and the vital.

The former looks upon life or vital force with all its physical mental and psychical phenomena as manifestations of the electric, magnetic and chemical activities of the physical-material elements composing the human organism. From this view point, life is a sort of "spontaneous combustion," or, as one scientist expressed it, a "succession of fermentations."

This materialistic conception of life, however, has already become obsolete among the more advanced biologists as a result of the discoveries of modern science, which are fast bridging the chasm between the material and the spiritual realms of being.

The vital conception of Life or Vital Force on the other hand, regards it as the primary force of all forces, coming from the central source of all power.

This force, which permeates, warms and animates the entire created universe, is the expression of the Divine Will, the Logos, the Word, of the Great Creative Intelligence. It is this Divine Energy which sets in motion the whirls in the ether, the electric corpuscles and ions that make up the different atoms and elements of matter.

These corpuscles and ions are positive and negative forms of electricity. Electricity is a form of energy. It is intelligent energy; otherwise it could not move with that unvarying wonderful precision in the electrons of the atoms as in the suns and planets of the sidereal universe.

If this supreme intelligence should withdraw its energy—the electrical charges (forms of energy)—and with it the atoms and elements, the entire material universe, would disappear in the flash of a moment.

From this it appears that crude matter, instead of being the source of life and of all its complicated mental and spiritual phenomena is only an expression of the Life Force, itself a manifestation of the Great Creative Intelligence which some call God, others Nature, the Oversoul, Brahma, Prana, etc., each one according to his understanding.

It is this supreme power and intelligence, acting in and through every atom, molecule, and cell in the human body, which is the true healer, this *"vis medicatrix naturae"* which always endeavors to repair, to heal, and to restore the perfect type. All that the physician can do is to remove obstructions and to establish normal condition within and about the patient, so that the power within can do its work to the best advantage.

In the final analysis, all things in Nature, from a fleeting thought or emotion to the hardest piece of diamond or platinum, are modes of motion or vibration. A few years ago physical science assumed that an atom was the smallest imaginable part of a given element of matter; that although infinitesimally small, it still represented solid matter. Now, in the light of better evidence, we have good reason to believe that there is no such thing as solid matter; that every atom is made up of charges of negative and positive electricity acting in and upon an omnipresent ether; that the difference between an atom of iron and of hydrogen, of any other element, consists solely in the number of electrical charges or corpuscles it contains, and on the velocity with which these vibrate around one another.

Thus the atom, which was thought to be the ultimate particle of solid matter, is found to be a little universe in itself in which corpuscles of electricity rotate or vibrate around one another like the suns and planets in the sidereal universe. This explains what we mean when we say life and matter are vibratory.

What we call "Inanimate Nature" is beautiful and orderly because it plays in tune with the score of the Symphony of Life. Man alone can play out of tune. This is his privilege, or his curse, as he chooses, by virtue of his freedom of choice and action.

We can now better understand the definitions of health and of disease, given in the catechism of Nature Cure as follows:

"Health is normal and harmonious vibration of the elements and forces composing the human entity on the physical, mental, moral, and spiritual planes of being, in conformity with the constructive principle of Nature applied to individual life."

"Disease is abnormal or inharmonious vibration of the elements and forces composing the human entity on one or more planes of being, in conformity with the destructive principle of Nature applied to individual life."

The question naturally arising here is, "Normal or abnormal vibration with what?" The answer is that the vibratory conditions of the organism must be in harmony with Nature's established harmonic relations in the physical, mental, moral, spiritual, and psychical realms of human life and action.

MENTAL MEDICINE

In "The Law of Mental Medicine," Thomson Jay Hudson, says:

"Like all the laws of nature, the law of mental medicine is universal in its application; and, like all the others, it is simple and easily comprehended. Granted that there is an intelligence that controls the functions of the body in health, it follows that it is the same power or energy that fails in case of disease. Failing, it requires assistance; and that is what all therapeutic agencies aim to accomplish. No intelligent physician of any school claims to be able to do more than to "assist nature" to restore normal conditions of the body.

That it is a mental energy that thus requires assistance, no one denies; for science teaches us that the whole body is made up of a confederation of intelligent entities, each of which performs its functions with an intelligence exactly adapted to the performance of its special duties as a member of the confederacy. There is, indeed, no life without mind, from the lowest unicellular organism up to man. It is, therefore, a mental energy that actuates every fibre of the body under all its conditions. That there is a central intelligence that controls each of those mind organisms, is self-evident.

Whether, as the materialistic scientists insist, this central intelligence is merely the sum of all the cellular intelligences of the bodily organism, or is an independent entity, capable of sustaining a separate existence after the body perishes, is a question that does not concern us in the pursuance of the present inquiry. It is sufficient for us to know that such an intelligence exists, and that, for the time being, it is the controlling energy that normally regulates the action of the myriad cells of which the body is composed.

It is, then, a mental organism that all therapeutic agencies are designed to energize, when, for any cause, it fails to perform its functions with reference to any part of the physical structure. It follows that mental therapeutic agencies are the primary and normal means of energizing the mental organism. That is to say, mental agencies operate more directly than any other, because more intelligibly, upon a mental organism; although physical agencies are by no means excluded, for all experience shows that a mental organism responds to physical as well as to mental stimuli. All that can be reasonably claimed is that, in therapeutics, a mental stimulus is necessarily more direct and more positive in its effects, other things being equal, than a physical stimulus can be, for the simple reason that it is intelligent on the one hand and intelligible on the other. It must be remarked, however, that it is obviously impossible wholly to eliminate mental suggestion even in the administration of material remedies. Extremists claim that the whole effect of material remedies is due to the factor of mental suggestion; but this seems to be untenable. The most that can be claimed with any degree of certainty is that Material remedies, when they are not in themselves positively injurious, are good and legitimate forms of suggestions, and, as such, are invested with a certain therapeutic potency, as in the administration of the placebo. It is also certain that, whether the remedies are material or mental, they must, directly or indirectly, energize the mental organism in control of the bodily functions. Otherwise the therapeutic effects produced cannot be permanent.

It follows that the therapeutic value of all remedial agencies, material or mental, is proportioned to their respective powers to produce the effect of stimulating the subjective mind to a state of normal activity, and directing its energies into appropriate channels. We know that suggestion fills this requirement more directly and positively than any other known therapeutic agent; and this is all that needs to be done for the restoration of health in any case outside of the domain of surgery. It is all that can be done. No power in the universe can do more than energize the mental organism that is the seat and source of health within the body. A miracle could do no more.

Professor Clouston, in his inaugural address to the Royal Medical Society in 1896, says:

"I would desire this evening to lay down or enforce a principle that is, I think, not sufficiently, and often not at all, considered in practical medicine and surgery. It is founded on a physiological basis, and it is of the highest practical importance. The principle is that the brain cortex, and especially the mental cortex, has such a position in the economy that it has to be reckoned with more or less as a factor for good or evil in all diseases of every organ, in all operations, and in all injuries. Physiologically the cortex is the great regulator of all functions, the ever-active controller of every organic disturbance. We know that every organ and every function are represented in the cortex, and are so represented that they all may be brought into the right relationship and harmony with each other, and so they all may be converted into a vital unity through it.

"Life and mind are the two factors of that organic unity that constitute a real animal organism. The mental cortex of man is the apex of the evolutionary pyramid, whose base is composed of the swarming pyramids of bacilli and other monocellular germs which we now see to be almost all-prevading in nature. It seems as if it has been the teleological aim of all evolution from the beginning. In it every other organ and function find their organic end. In histological structure—so far as we yet know this—it far exceeds all other organs in complexity.

"When we fully know the structure of each neuron, with its hundreds of fibres and its thousands of dendrites, and the relation of one neuron to another, when we can demonstrate the cortical apparatus for universal intercommunication of nervous energy, with its absolute solidarity, its partial localisation, and its wondrous arrangements for mind, motion, sensibility, nutrition, repair, and drainage—when we fully know all this, there will be no further question of the dominance of the brain cortex in the organic hierarchy, nor of its supreme importance in disease.''

''The Lancet'' records a case of Dr. Barkas of a woman (58) with supposed disease of every organ, with pains everywhere, who tried every method of cure, but was at last experimentally cured by mental therapeutics pure and simple. Assured that death would result from her state, and that a certain medicine would infallibly cure her, provided it was administered by an experienced nurse, one tablespoonful of pure distilled water was given her at 7, 12, 5 and 10, to the second with scrupulous care; and in less than three weeks all pain ceased, all diseases were cured, and remained so. This is a valuable experiment as excluding every material remedy whatever, and proving that it is the mental factor alone that cures; however, it may be generally associated with material remedies.

Dr. Morrison, of Edinburgh, discovered that a lady who had constant violent hysterical attacks had given her hand to one man and her heart to another. A little direct common-sense talk in this case formed an agreeable substitute for the distilled water in the other, and the patient never had another attack.

Many seem to think that only nervous or functional diseases are cured by Mental or Spiritual methods, but Alfred T. Schofield, M. D., tells in "The Force of Mind:"

In one long list of 250 published cases of disease cured we find five "consumption," one "diseased hip," five "abscess," three "dyspepsia," four "internal complaint," two "throat ulcer," seven "nervous debility," nine "rheumatism," five diseased heart," two "withered arm," four "bronchitis," three "cancer," two paralyzed arm," three "weak eyes," one "ruptured spine," five "pains in the head." And these are the results in one year at one small chapel in the north of London.

What about the "cures" at home and Continental spas, with their eternal round of sulphur and iron waters and baths?

Does the doctor attached to the spa, in his heart of hearts believe that all the cures which in these cases he cheerfully certifies to are effected by the waters, or even the waters and the diet, or even the waters and the diet and the air; or does he not think there must be a "something else" as well? And to come nearer home and into the centre of all things, and the chamber of all his secrets: In his own consulting room and in his own practice, is not the physician brought face to face with cures, aye, and diseases, too, the cause of which he cannot account for; and is he not often surprised to find a continuation of the same treatment originated by the local practitioners is, when continued by his august self, efficacious? And is not the local practitioner not only surprised but disgusted as well to find such is the case?

Does any practical medical man, after all, really doubt these mental powers? Is he not aware of the ingredient "faith," which, if added to his prescriptions, makes them often all-powerful for good? Does he know experimentally the value of strongly asserting that the medicine will produce such and such effects as a powerful means of securing them?

If, then, this power is so well known, why in the name of common sense is it ignored? It has its laws of action, its limitations, its powers for good and for evil; would it not clearly help the medical student if these were indicated to him by his lawful teachers, instead of his gleaning them uncertainly from the undoubted successes of the large army of irregulars?

We are, however, inclined to think that, after all, a silent revolution is slowly taking place in the minds of medical men, and that our present text-books on disease, content with merely prescribing any mental cure in a single line as unworthy of serious consideration, will in time be replaced by others containing views more worthy of the century in which we live.''

ORTHOBIOSIS.

Virgil says: "Happy is he who has found the cause of things."

It was Metchnikoff who tried, after his investigations into the physical, to apply ethics to life, so that life might be lived to the full, which is the true wisdom. He called this condition orthobiosis. He held that the end of science is to rid the world of its scourges, through hygiene and other measures of prophylaxis.

Our manner of life, says Mme. Metchnikoff, transcribing her husband's idea, will have to be modified and directed according to rational and scientific data if we are to run through the normal cycle of life—orthobiosis. The pursuit of that goal will ever influence the basis of morals. Orthobiosis cannot be accessible to all until knowledge, rectitude and solidarity increase among men, and until social conditions are kinder.

Like all faculties, faith has a center through which it functions—the pineal gland. Faith is therefore physical, just as disease may be spiritual; spirit and body are but parts of a glorious whole. The cure of disease requires the use of Cosmic Force; and who shall say that that force—wheth-er we call it God, Nature, Oversoul, Brah-ma, *Vis Medicatrix Naturae, Prana, Logos,* Divine Will does not manifest itself through material means, as well as spirit-ual?

"Plato," Dr. Butler tells us, "said that man is a plant rooted in heaven, and we agree to this, that he is also rooted in the earth." In fact, man may be said to have two origins, one earthly and physical, the other spiritual, though the former orig-inates in the latter—so that ultimately the origin is one . . . .

"Man is an organism. De Quincey defines an organism as a group of parts which act upon the whole, the whole in turn acting upon all the parts. This is simple and true.

"It is paradoxical that mind, though a principal and usually a determining part of a human organism's actions and reactions, has by formal medicine been disregarded as a primary cause in pretty much all of those bodily disorders which are not produced by contagion. But of late years autointoxication and disturbances of the ductless glands have come into increased consideration. Their operations are being gradually traced to origins beyond the physical body, and definitely located in states of mind. These states are coming within the scope of diagnostics; enlightened medical art brings them under treatment.''

Recognition of the influence of mind upon the body was recognized even of old, as far back as Hippocrates, and probably anterior to him. Mondeville, in the 14th century, approved of the custom of reciting certain verses of the psalms when taking medicine; nor was he averse to pilgrimages undertaken in search of health—he held that no harm could be done, while the potentialities of good were great. The value of the physical exercise in going on a pil-

grimage, usually on foot, with most of the
time spent in the open air, need scarcely be
pointed out. Many a cure of lethargy and
obesity in the middle ages and after owed
its efficacy to the insistence of famous phy-
sicians that the patients, no matter how
wealthy or high-born, were to come from
their dwellings on foot, in all humility, refusing to extend treatment otherwise.

Ignatius of Loyola is credited with saying: "Do everything you can with the idea
that everything depends on you, and then
hope for results just as if everything depended on God."

It will be found that the sanest, most
catholic and liberal exponents of each
school of healing generously admit the
value of other schools and the limitations
of their own. The responsible healer of
the future, who truly respects his honor-
able calling, will employ all beneficial, constructive agencies at the disposal of science. Thus, we have an eminent occultist
saying:

"In cases of misplacement, dislocation,
or broken bones, the quickest way to ob-

tain relief is to send for a competent physician or anatomist and have an adjustment made of the injured member or organ. In cases of disruptions of blood-vessels or muscles, a surgeon's aid should be immediately sought; not because mind is unable to cure any or all of these cases, but because of the fact that at the present time, even among educated people, mind is many times impotent through misuse or non-use. Mental treatment should follow these physical treatments in order to obviate unnecessary suffering and to obtain rapid recovery."

We can not do better than to quote, Sir William Osler, Bt., M. D., F. R. S.:

"The salvation of science lies in a recognition of a new philosophy—the *scientia scientiarum* of which Plato speaks: 'Now when all these studies reach the point of intercommunion and connection with one another and come to be considered in their mutual affinities, then, I think, and not till then, will the pursuit of them have a value.'" "The Old Humanities and the New Science."

Scientists assume that there is one sub-stance only, and therefore their deduced science is the science of that substance, and none other; and yet they are confronted with the fact that their one substance is differentiated, and that when they come to the finest degree thereof, as for instance bioplasm, we are brought face to face with the operation of higher laws than they are familiar with, or can adequately ex-plain.

Many scientists, however, with a broad-er view, are beginning to glimpse a ''fourth dimension,'' and recognize the fact that there may be degrees of matter which are utterly beyond their chemical tests and microscopic lens.

But a new day is dawning, the telephone, the telegraph and the wireless are now coming into general use and it is now pos-sible to make use of every avenue of infor-mation and knowledge. It is therefore but a question of time when the sick will have the benefit of all that is known in the art of healing.

The physician frequently loses his patient because he refuses to recognize the spiritual nature of the patient, and that because of his spiritual nature there are certain fundamental laws governing in the spiritual world, and that these laws continue to operate whether he recognizes them or not, and the metaphysician frequently loses his patient because he refuses to recognize that the body of the patient is the material manifestation of the spirit within, and that the condition of the body is but an expression of the spirit.

But all this iconoclasm is but the result of a certain conservatism which is both human and natural. With the wisdom which the years are bringing there will soon be no one who cannot see that the germ is not only the cause of disease but the result of disease, that bacteria is the result of impure water not the cause of impure water, and so with everything else.

What we can see, handle or touch are never causes, but always effects, and if it is our purpose to simply substitute one form of distress for another we shall continue to deal with effects and effects only, but if it is our purpose to bring about a remedy, we shall seek the cause by which alone every effect is brought into existence, and this cause will never be found in the world of effects.

In the new era, abnormal, mental and emotional conditions will be immediately detected and corrected. Tissue in process of destruction will be eliminated or reconstructed by the constructive methods at the disposal of the physician. Abnormal lesions will be corrected by manipulative treatment, but above and beyond all of this will be the primary and essential idea, the idea upon which all results will depend and that is that no inharmonious or destructive thought shall be allowed to reach the patient, that every thought for him or about him shall be constructive, for every physician, every nurse, every attendant, every relative will eventually come to know that thoughts are spiritual things, which are ever seeking manifestation, and that as soon as they find fertile soil they begin to germinate.

Not all thoughts find expression in the objective world and especially in the health and environment of the patient. This is because not all patients are responsive, but when the patient finds that these invisible guests come laden with precious gifts, they will be given a royal welcome. This welcome will be subconscious because the thoughts of others are received subconsciously.

The conscious mind receives thought only through the organs of perception, which are its method of contact with the objective world; which are the five senses, seeing, hearing, feeling, tasting and smelling.

Subconscious thought is received by any organ of the body affected and think of the mechanism which has been provided and which can and does objectify the thought received. First the millions of cell chemists ready and waiting to carry out all instructions received. Next the complete system of communication, consisting of the vast sympathetic nervous system reaching every fibre of the being and ready to respond to the slightest emotion of joy or fear, of hope or despair, of courage or impotence.

Next the complete manufacturing plant consisting of a series of glands wherein are manufactured all the secretions necessary for the use of the chemists in carrying out the instructions which have been given.

Then there is the complete digestive tract wherein food, water and air are converted into blood, bone, skin, hair and nails.

Then there is the supply department which constantly sends a supply of Oxygen, Nitrogen and Ether into every part of the being, and the wonder of it all is that this Ether holds in solution everything necessary for the use of the chemist, for the Ether holds in pure form, and food, water, and air in the secondary form every element necessary for the use of the chemist in the production of a perfect man.

Why then do not these chemists produce a perfect specimen of manhood? The reply is simple, the prescriptions which consist of thoughts received by the subconscious call for nothing of the kind, in fact, they usually call for exactly the reverse.

The subconscious is also provided with a complete equipment for the elimination of waste and useless material as well as a complete repair department. In addition to this there is a complete system of wireless whereby it is connected with every other subconscious entity in existence.

We are not usually conscious of the operation of this wireless, but the same thing is true concerning the operation of the Marconi System. There may be messages of all kinds all about us, but unless we make use of an amplifier, we receive no message, and so with our subconscious wireless. Unless we try to co-ordinate the conscious and the subconscious we fail to realize that **the subconscious is** constantly receiving messages of some kind and just as constantly objectifying the messages in our life and environment.

This then is the mechanism devised and planned by the Creator, Himself, and it has been placed under the supervision of the subconscious instead of the conscious mind, but let us not forget that the subconscious mind with all of its wonderful mechanism can be controlled and dominated by the conscious mind when it becomes attuned to the Universal Mind, where all that is, or ever was, or ever shall be is held in solution waiting to come forth and manifest in form.

Every day that is born into the world comes like a burst of music, and rings itself all the day through; and thou shalt make of it a dance, a dirge or a life march, as thou wilt.

—Carlyle.

BIOCHEMISTRY

Biochemistry is a science, whose concern is with vital processes, and which has availed itself of the cell theory and of the principle of the infinite divisibility of matter. It also makes use of the homeopathic dose. The dose must be proportionate to the patient, the cell; for, as Virchow has pointed out, "the essence of disease is the cell, changed pathogenically." -

Dr. Schuessler, the originater of Biochemistry, arrived at his conclusions by studying the elements, nature, and functions of human blood. The cells receive their sustenance, their life-supply, from the blood and lymph, which, in their turn, derive their supply from the elements taken in as food. Normalcy in the supply of these elements means health; any deviation, a disturbance of health.

Dr. Schuessler placed the number of mineral combinations in the human body at twelve; in the last edition, 1895, he reduced the number to eleven. These all-necessary cell-salts are:

Potassium Chloride, Potassium Phosphate, Potassium Sulphate, Sodium Chloride, Sodium Phosphate, Sodium Sulphate, Phosphate of Lime, Fluoride of Lime, Phosphate of Magnesia, Phosphate of Iron, Silica.

Milk contains all these elements; other foods can give them in combination. Cremation reduces the body to these elements.

Each kind of cell depends upon a different salt, or combination of salts, for its food; a lack of any of these salts is shown by certain symptoms; the proper tissue salts, in right proportions are given to remove the symptoms, since a removal of the symptoms implies a removal of the need, or disease, in the cell.

It must be remembered, however, that the cells are not fed, they feed themselves; and any attempt to compel them to accept more than they require causes disaster. They voluntarily accept what is necessary and they reject what they do not need.

The difference in the cells consists in the kind and quality of the inorganic tissue salts of which they are composed.

Health, therefore, requires the requisite quantity of cell salts, and a lack of some one of these organic tissue salts results in imperfect cell action and diseased tissue.

The controlling principle which underlies every manifestation of form may be epitomized as follows: "In the apportionment and grouping of the elements that constitute a thing lies the cause, not only of the form, but also of its functions and qualities."

Dr. Charles W. Littlefield, M. D., the author of "The Beginning and the Way of Life," gives some very beautiful illustrations of the application of this law. in the chapter on the "Elements and Compounds of Nature," in which he says:

"Within the scope and application of this principle of grouping of electrons, as the law of origin of elements, molecules, tissues, organs and forms, will be found a practical solution to every problem in biology from the origin and differentiation of species to every modification of form and configuration of outline that mark individuals with characteristic personalities, both physical and mental . . . . It is well known in chemistry that the molecule is the smallest part of any substance that can exist separately and still retain its properties. Since the nature of the molecule is determined by the polarities, number and arrangement of the "electrons" which compose it, and since all structures in the mineral, vegetable and animal kingdoms are molecular, it follows that in the last analysis the grouping and apportionment of negative and positive "electrons" in the molecule determine in turn the nature and physical conditions of the form, whether it be perfect or imperfect. Deformity, personal likes and dislikes, are only questions of being "electronically" balanced or unbalanced, through supply or lack of supply of the forms of molecules that compose the organism. Only the spirit-mind-image of man, however, can make this grouping of molecules for the perfecting of a human form. To bring humanity to a state of primitive perfection, therefore, not only must the same material, prepared in the same manner, be supplied, but the environment of forces must be the same as those employed by the Creative Spirit in the beginning.

"Since then, we are able to trace every elemental form of matter back to some definite grouping of negative and positive electrons, that is, through varying numbers and arrangements of these; and since we find life manifesting through various forms as determined by different molecular groupings—by law of composition—and since it is rational to place Divine Mind behind this physical process, we are justified in assuming that Divine Mind—Images of living things preceded their physical development. Therefore, in the ultimate science of being, idealism is more probable than materialism. But, while mind may thus exist alone there in the realm of cause, here in the realm of phenomena,we always have a psycho-physical parallelism, a realism, where everything must be explained by mind and matter, but by neither alone. While the spiritual entity which constitutes the real self may well be assumed to be akin to the Supreme Mind, being a particular mind-image thereof in the line of descent, having power of choice and therefore of independent action, it is unquestionably limited, like that of the player by his instrument, by bodily conditions.

In "The Chemistry of Life," Dr. George W. Carey says:

"So-called disease is neither a "person, place nor thing."

The symptoms of sensation, called disease, are the results of lacking material—a deficiency in the dynamic molecules that carry on the orderly procedure of life. The effect of the deficiency causes unpleasant sensations, pains, exudations, swellings; or overheated tissue caused by increased motion of blood.

The increased motion is the effort nature, or chemical law, makes to restore equilibrium with the diminished molecules of blood builders. By the law of the conservation of energy the increased motion is changed to heat. We call this effect fever.

Biochemistry means the Chemistry of Life, or the union of inorganic and organic substances whereby new compounds are formed.

In its relation to so-called disease this system uses the inorganic salts, known as Cell-salts, or tissue builders.

The constituent parts of man's body are perfect principles, namely, oxygen, hydrogen, carbon, lime, iron, potash, soda, silica, magnesia, etc. These elements, gases, etc., are perfect *per se,* but may be endlessly diversified in combination as may the planks, bricks, or stones with which a building is to be erected.

Symptoms, called disease, disappear or cease to manifest when the food called for is furnished.

The human body is a receptacle for a storage battery, and will always run right while the chemicals are present in proper quantity and combination, as surely as an automobile will run when charged and supplied with the necessary ingredients to vibrate or cause motion.

The cell-salts are found in all our food, and are thus carried into the blood, where they carry on the process of life, and by the law of Chemical Affinity keep the human form, bodily functions, materialized. When a deficiency occurs in any of these workers through a non-assimilation of food, poor action of liver or digestive process, dematerialization of the body commences. So disease is a deficiency in some of the chemical constituents that carry on the chemistry of life.

Biochemists have shown that food does not form blood, but simply furnishes the mineral base by setting free the inorganic or cell-salts contained in all food stuff. The organic part, oil, fibrin, albumen, etc., contained in food is burned or digested in the stomach and intestinal tract to furnish motive power to operate the human machine and draw air into lungs, thence into arteries, i. e., air carriers.

Therefore, it is clearly proven that air (spirit) unites with the minerals and forms blood, proving that the oil, albumen, etc., found in blood, is created every breath.

Increase the rate of activity of the brain cells by supplying more of the dynamic molecules of the blood known as mineral or cell -salts of lime, potash, sodium, iron, magnesia, silica, and we see mentally, truths that we could not sense at lower or natural rates of motion, although the lower rate may manifest ordinary health.

Natural man, or natural things must be raised from the level of nature to supernatural, in order to realize new concepts that lie waiting for recognition.

By this regenerative process millions of dormant cells of the brain are resurrected and set in operation, and then man no longer "sees through a glass darkly," but with the Eye of Spiritual understanding."

"This above all: To thine own self be true,
And it must follow, as the night the day,
Thou canst not then be false to any man."

" 'Tis shown in Life's puzzles and sorrowings,
'Tis taught by remorse with its secret stings,
That he who grief to another brings,
One day, in his turn, must weep.

"From the past doth the present eternally spring;
You may sow what you will, but tomorrow will bring
You the harvest, to show you the manner of thing
Is the seed you have chosen to sow!"

SUGGESTION.

Mr. C. Harry Brooks tells of a very interesting and instructive visit to the clinic of Dr. Emile Coue in a book entitled the *Practice of Auto-suggestion,* published by Dodd, Mead & Co. The clinic is situated in a pleasant garden attached to Dr. Coue's house at the end of the rue Jeanne d'Arc, in Nancy. He states that when he arrived the room reserved for patients was already crowded, but in spite of that, eager newcomers constantly tried to gain entrance. The window sills on the ground floor were beset and a dense knot had formed in the door. The patients had occupied every available seat and were sitting on camp stools and folding chairs.

He then tells of the many remarkable cures which Dr. Coue proceeded to effect by no other means than suggestion to the patient that the power of healing lies within the patient himself. There was also a children's clinic in charge of Mademoiselle Kauffmant who devotes her entire time to this work.

Mr. Brooks thinks that "Coue's" discoveries may profoundly affect our life and education because it teaches us that the burdens of life are, at least in a large measure, of our own creating. We reproduce in ourselves and in our circumstances the thoughts of our minds. It goes further, it offers us a means by which we can change these thoughts when they are evil and foster them when they are good, so producing a corresponding betterment in our individual life. But the process does not end with the individual. The thoughts of society are realized in social conditions, the thoughts of humanity in world conditions. What would be the attitude towards our social and international problems of a generation nurtured from infancy in the knowledge and practice of auto-suggestion? If each person found happiness in his own heart, would the illusory greed for possession survive? The acceptance of auto-suggestion entails a change of attitude, a revaluation of life. If we stand with our faces westward we see nothing but clouds and darkness, yet by a simple turn of the head we bring the wide panorama of the sunrise into view.''

The New York Times, under date of Aug. 6, 1922, published an excellent likeness of Emile Coue and a review of his work by Van Buren Thorne, M. D. He says that the keynote to the system of treatment of mental and physical ills devised and elaborated by Emile Coue of Nancy, France, can be described in a single paragraph:

''The individual is possessed of two minds, called the conscious and the unconscious. The latter is referred to by some psychologists as the subconscious mind, and is literally the humble and obedient servant of the conscious mind. The unconscious mind is the director and overseer of our internal economy. By means of its activities the processes of digestion and assimilation of foods are carried on, repairs are made, wastes are eliminated, our vital organs function and life itself persists. When the thought arises in the conscious mind that extra efforts toward the repair of some deficiency, either physical or mental are needed, all the individual has to do, in the opinion of Dr. Coue, is audibly to enunciate that thought in the form of a direct suggestion to the unconscious mind, and that humble obedient servant immediately, and without questioning the dictates of its conscious master, proceeds to obey instructions.''

Dr. Coue, Mr. Brooks, and large numbers of persons of repute in France, England, and elsewhere in Europe, have declared that the results in many cases under their direct observation have been nothing short of marvelous. Those who have not witnessed the benefits of this form of treatment—hence may incline to be skeptical—are more likely to give attention to what follows when they are informed of three facts regarding the Nancy practice. First, Dr. Coue has never accepted a penny for his treatments in the many years of his ministration; second, he is in the habit of explaining to his patients that he possesses no healing powers, has never healed a person in his life, and that they must find the instruments of their own well-being in themselves; third, that any individual can treat himself without consulting any other person.

It may be added that a child who is capable of comprehending the fact of the conscious and subconscious mind, and is competent to issue orders from one to the other, is quite capable of the self-administration of the treatment.

"For what man knoweth the things of a man save the spirit of the man which is in him?" Mr. Brooks quotes from First Corinthians for his title page. Doubtless this was selected as an apt biblical reference to the existence of the conscious and unconscious minds. But neither the treatment, nor this book about it, dwells at length upon any possible religious significance of the methods employed or the results obtained.

The single thing that has contributed largely to the recent rapid spread of knowledge concerning Dr. Coue's method of practice at Nancy is his insistence upon the benefits to be derived from the frequent repetition of this formula: "Day by day, in every way, I'm getting better and better." As I remarked, no great stress is laid upon the religious significance of his alleged cures; yet, says Mr. Brooks, "religious minds who wish to associate the formula with God's care and protection might do so after this fashion: 'Day by day, in every way, by the help of God, I'm getting better and better.'" The secret of success in the treatment is to so beget confidence in the conscious mind that what it repeats is accepted at its face value by the unconscious mind, and as Mr. Brooks puts it: "Every idea which enters the conscious mind, if it is accepted by the unconscious, is transformed by it into a reality and forms henceforth a permanent element in our life."

But let us see how this book came to be written, and then watch Dr. Coue at work.

Mr. Brooks is an Englishman who became interested in Dr. Coue's work at Nancy and went there to observe it at first hand. In his foreword to the volume, Dr. Coue says that Mr. Brooks visited him for several weeks last summer, and that he was the first Englishman who came to Nancy with the express purpose of studying methods of conscious auto-suggestion. He attended Dr. Coue's consultations and obtained a full mastery of the method. Then the two men threshed out a good deal of the theory on which the treatment rests.

Dr. Coue says that Mr. Brooks skillfully seized on the essentials and that he has put them forward in the volume in a manner that seems to him both simple and clear.

"It is a method," says Dr. Coue, "which every one should follow—the sick to obtain healing, the healthy to prevent the coming of disease in the future. By its practice we can insure for ourselves, all our lives long, an excellent state of health, both of the mind and the body."

Now let us enter Dr. Coue's clinic with Mr. Brooks. Back of the house there is a pleasant garden with flowers, strawberry beds, and fruit-laden trees. Groups of patients occupy the garden seats. There are two brick buildings—the waiting and consultation rooms. These are crowded with patients—men, women and children.

Coue immediately proceeds to his work. Patient No. 1 is a man of middle age and frail. He can scarcely walk, and his head, legs and arms shake with an exaggerated tremor. His daughter supports him. Coue invites him to arise and walk. Aided by a stick, he staggers across the floor a few steps.

Coue tells him he is going to get better, and adds: "You have been sowing bad seed in your Unconscious; now you will sow good seed. The power by which you have produced such ill-effects will in the future produce equally good ones."

"Madame," he tells a woman who breaks into a torrent of complaint, "you think too much about your ailments, and in thinking of them you create fresh ones."

He tells a girl with headaches, a youth with inflamed eyes, and a laborer with varicose veins, that auto-suggestion should bring complete relief. He comes to a neurasthenic girl who is making her third visit to the clinic and who has been practicing the method at home for ten days. She says she is getting better. She can now eat heartily, sleep soundly, and is beginning to enjoy life.

A big peasant, formerly a blacksmith, next engages his attention. He says he has not been able to raise his right arm above the level of his shoulder for nearly ten years. Coue predicts a complete cure. For forty minutes he keeps on with the interrogation of patients.

Then he pays attention to those who have come to tell him of the benefits they have received. Here is a woman who has had a painful swelling in her breast, diagnosed by the doctor (in Coue's opinion, wrongly), as cancerous. She says that, with three weeks' treatment, she has completely recovered. Another has overcome her anaemia and has gained nine pounds in weight. A third says he has been cured of varicose ulcer; while a fourth, a lifelong stammerer, announces a complete cure in one sitting.

Coue now turns to the former blacksmith and says: "For ten years you have been thinking that you could not lift your arm above your shoulder; consequently, you have not been able to do so, for whatever we think becomes true for us. Now think: 'I can lift it.'"

The man looks doubtful, says half-heartedly, "I can," makes an effort, and says it hurts.

"Keep it up,' Coue commands in a tone of authority, "and think 'I can, I can!' Close your eyes and repeat with me as fast as you can, '*ça passe, ça passe.*'"

After half a minute of this, Coue says, "Now think well that you can lift your arm."

"I can," says the man with conviction and proceeds to raise it to full height, where he holds it in triumph for all to see.

"My friend," observes Dr. Coue quietly. "You are cured."

"It is marvelous," says the bewildered blacksmith, "I believe it."

"Prove it," says Coue, "by hitting me on the shoulder," whereupon the blows fall in regular sequence.

"Enough," cautions Coue, wincing from the sledge-hammer blows. "Now you can go back to your anvil."

Now he turns to patient No. 1, the tottering man. The sufferer seems inspired with confidence by what he has seen. Under Coue's instructions he takes control of himself, and in a few minutes he is walking about with ease.

"When I get through with the clinic," says Coue, "you shall come for a run in the garden."

And so it happens; very soon this patient is trotting around the enclosure at five miles an hour.

Coue then proceeds to the formulation of specific suggestions. The patients close their eyes and he speaks in a low, monotonous voice. Here is an example:

"Say to yourself that all the words I am about to utter will be fixed, imprinted and engraved in your minds; that they will remain fixed, imprinted and engraven there, so that without your will and knowledge, without your being in any way aware of what is taking place, you yourself and your whole organism will obey them. I tell you first that every day, three times a day, morning, noon and evening, at meal times, you will be hungry; that is to say, you will feel that pleasant sensation which makes us think and say: "How I should like something to eat.' You will then eat with excellent appetite, enjoying your food, but you will never eat too much. You will eat the right amount, neither too much nor too little, and you will know intuitively when you have sufficient. You will masticate your food thoroughly, transforming it into a smooth paste before swallowing it. In these conditions you will digest it well, and so feel no discomfort of any kind either in the stomach or in the intestines. Assimilation will be perfectly performed, and your organism will make the best possible use of the food to create blood, muscle, strength, energy, in a word—Life.''

"They (Dr. Coue and Mlle. Kauff-mant)," says Mr. Brooks, ''have placed not only their private means, but their whole life at the service of others. Neither ever accepts a penny-piece for the treatments they give, but I have never seen Coue refuse to give a treatment at however awkward an hour the subject may have asked it. The fame of the school has now spread to all parts, not only France, but of Europe and America. Coue's work has assumed such proportions that his time is taken up often to the extent of fifteen or sixteen hours a day. He is a living monument to the efficacy of "Induced Auto-suggestion.''

In "Regeneration," Mr. Weltmer says:

"The last battle in which the race is engaged is now on. It is not a battle of cannon and sword, but it is a conflict of ideas. It is not going to be destructive, but constructive. It will not be a destroying warfare, but a fulfilling. It will not promote discord, but will insure harmony. It will not knit the human family together in combinations and associations, lodges and congregations, but will individualize the race, and each person will stand alone, recognizing within himself all the potentialities that exist, recognizing within himself all the Divine principles, constituting a part of the perfect whole.

"When man sees himself thus, he will see this kingdom within, is not within him only, but within all men. We must assume that the power to do, to act, or to perform the work we give our minds to do, exists in the mind; but before we entrust the mind with this work, we must have a clear conception of what is to be done. In order to regenerate the body we must conclude or assume to be true, that the power to generate life and health is in us; we must know where it is generated and how to generate it.

"Could we but comprehend it, could the veil of ignorance that enshrouds us be lifted, and we be allowed to look into the storehouse of knowledge, such as the prophet or seer was allowed to look upon, could we but climb where Moses stood, and view the landscape o'er, could we experience what Paul did during the time when he says: 'I know not whether I was in the body or out of the body,' we would be able to comprehend what he means when he says: 'Eye hath not seen, nor ear heard, nor hath it entered into the heart of man, the glory that shall be revealed in us.' "

The brain is an organ through which we communicate our thoughts to other organs in our bodies, and receive impressions from the outside through the mediums of the senses. Great men have by great thoughts developed a finer quality of brain than others; this leads people to think that the great mind was the outgrowth of the fine brain, when if they will look upon the brain as any other organ of the perishable body they will see that it is but the organ through which the mind finds expression.

All attainments come in their regular order, as orderly as the movements of the sun and planets; first we desire, second we believe, third we try the belief, fourth we have knowledge.

We entertain a belief, and the belief comes into our minds and controls us. A man in the throes of poverty can throw off the shackles, if he can add to his belief.

A suggestion, to be a controlling influence, must be a positive suggestion left undisturbed; it must be regarded by the person entertaining it as a fixture in his life; not subject to change or modification.

Still another method of making an application of the principle of suggestion is described by Mr. J. R. Seaward, of Hamilton, Mont. He says:

"I am a man 36 years of age and have a family, and they rejoice with me that I am free from the use of tobacco. I chewed, or rather ate the weed for 15 years. Didn't mean to form the habit when I started in, but thought that it was conducive to my growth from youth to manhood. After the habit had grown on me for several years unresisted, I discovered that I was in the grip of a slowly but surely growing octopus that had me freely within its embrace, and I was helpless to release myself. I had followed carpenter and shop woodwork for a trade, and all woodworkers know there is something about lumber that makes a man want to use tobacco. When I got so that I had to chew all the time and the strongest I could get and then was not satisfied, I began to wonder where I was headed for. Slowly the idea that I was a slave to the weed dawned on me and I began to think about cutting down on it, or out altogether.

"I will now explain to you the way in which Friend Wife broke me of a vile habit and convinced us both of the marvelous power of Suggestion when properly applied.

"At about the time that I struck bottom, there came to my notice some literature, telling of the power of directed thought, and I became interested in the study of that, and also in some inspirational literature which later came to my notice. I was rather skeptical at first, but as I read and thought and commenced to look for proof in the events of our daily lives and in our environment, the truth commenced to dawn upon me. I began to see and know that life manifestations were fed from within and grew from within, and if the within be in a state of decay, it invariably showed without. In fact, I know now that 'The Man of Gallilee,' said something when He said, 'As a man thinketh in his heart, so is he.' If he thinks himself a slave to tobacco or other obnoxious habits, so is he. He must think himself free to remain free, once he has gained freedom.

"But to think one's self away from a habit that clings as close as thought itself, is a hard matter unaided. At the time we tried suggestion for the elimination of my tobacco habit I slept in one bedroom with one of the children and wife slept in another bedroom with our then youngest boy, about eight months old. As often is the case she had to be up at times during the night to wait on the baby and it was at those times that she gave me mental treatments while I was asleep.

"It isn't necessary to be in the same room, though it is all right if it happens to be the case. While I was sleeping she would visualize herself or mentally project herself as though she was standing or kneeling beside my bed and speaking to me. Her suggestions were of a constructive and positive nature rather than of negative. It went something like this: 'You are now desiring freedom from the tobacco habit; you are free and desire and enjoy mastery more than indulgence; tomorrow you will want only about half the normal amount of tobacco and each day it will be less until you are free within a week and shall never have any more craving for tobacco. You are Master and free.'

"She made the above suggestion (in substance) to me each time that she was awake during the night and I do pledge on oath that within six days from the time she started treatment I had completely quit craving tobacco, and quit using it.

That has been several months ago, and to-day I am more master of my habits of thought and word and deed than ever before in my life. I have changed from an under-weight, nervous wreck to a full-weight, healthful, strong, energetic, and clear-thinking man, and everyone who knew me remarks how differently I look and act and seem. Since that time, I have followed the study and the practice of constructive and directed thinking.''

You know that in wireless telegraphy or telephony they use an instrument called the tuning coil that vibrates in harmony with an electrical wave or vibration of a certain length. It is in tune with that particular tune of wave and consequently they are in harmony and allow the vibration to go on to the other receiving instrument unhindered. Yet there may be other wireless vibrations of a higher or lower ''tune'' or key passing at the same time, yet only those in harmony are registered by the receiver.

Now our minds are just about the same way only we regulate our "tuning" coil by our Will power. We can tune our minds to low-vibration thoughts such as the animal-impulses of nature, or we can "tune" them to thoughts of an educational or mental nature, or we can, after some qualifications are met, "tune" ourselves to receive purely spiritual thought vibrations. This power constitutes the Divine power that is given to man. Of course you will readily see that there never was a primitive hut or modern mansion built without the application of this principle of directed constructive thinking and visualization.

The backbone of salesmanship of all kinds is the understanding and skillful use of suggestion. When cleverly used it tends to relax one's conscious attention and warm up and quicken the Desire, until a favorable response is gained. Window displays and counter displays as well as illustrated advertising all rely on the power to drive a suggestion into the very center of Desire, where it grows to the point of action if in harmony with the thought vibration of the Desire. If the desire does not recognize or is not in harmony with the suggestion it is as "seed that has fallen upon stony ground," and is without harvest of action.

Thought and action do produce material results as is easily verified in the builder and his plans—the dressmaker and her pattern, or the school and its product, all in harmony with the leading constructive thought. The quality of thought determines the measure of success in life.

All truly wise thoughts have been thought already thousands of times; but to make them truly ours, we must think them over again honestly, till they take root in our personal experience.

—Goethe.

PSYCHO-ANALYSIS.

"Canst thou not minister to a mind diseased," asked *Macbeth* of the *Doctor*—but the passage is so strikingly fitting, so prophetically explanatory of psychoanalysis, that it must be given in full:

Macbeth: Canst thou not minister to a mind diseased.

Pluck from the memory a rooted sorrow.

Raze out the written troubles of the brain.

And with some sweet oblivious antidote Cleanse the stuff'd bossom of that perilous stuff

Which weight upon the heart?

Doctor: Therein the patient must minister to himself.

There is hardly a person today exempt from some form of phobia, or fear, whose origin may date so far back as to be lost among the shadows of childhood; hardly a person is free from some aversion, or "complex," whose effects are a matter of daily occurrence, despite the will of the victim. In a sense, the subconsciousness has never forgotten the incident, and still harbours the unpleasant memory of it; the consciousness, however, in an attempt to protect our dignity, or vanity, whichever you prefer, may evolve some apparent, better reason than the original one. Thus complexes are formed. Brontephobia, or fear of thunder, was brought about in the case of one patient by hearing a cannon go off very near her when she was a child; a fact which had been "forgotten" for years; to confess to such a fear, even to one's self, would have been childish—and fear to the somewhat more dignified cause of thunder. Needless to say, it is such disguises of the memories which make difficult the labor of the psychoanalyst to pluck from the memory a rooted sorrow, to raze out the written troubles of the brain, its "traumas" or the original shocks. And when we remember that Psyche in Greek means not only the mind, but the soul, we can better understand Shakespeare's amazing grasp of psychology when he speaks not only of the "mind diseased," but of "that perilous stuff which weighs upon the heart."

We all have these complexes, in forms ranging from the mild to the severe; sitophobia, the aversion to certain foods; claustophobia, the fear of locked doors—to which the fear of open spaces forms a striking contrast; stage-fright; touching wood and other superstitions—a thorough list would indeed be a very long one.

For the greater part, the patient must minister to himself—with the help of the skilled psychoanalyst. In some cases elaborate processes are needed, and the use of psychometers and other delicate registering devices enlisted; but usually, the procedure is a simple one. The subject of investigation is made comfortable physically, and put in a quiet mood; he is then told to utter whatever may come into his mind in connection with his complex—with occasional promptings and questions from the

psychoanalyst. Sooner or later the association of ideas will bring to the surface
the original, cause or experience, which
had become "rooted," submerged; very
often the mere explanation will suffice to
eradicate the obsession.

But there is another group of disorders,
hysteria, which may partake both of the
physical and the psychical, or where either
state may induce the other. Richard In-
galese in his "History and Power of
Mind," has summed up the matter very
clearly: "Disease may be divided into two
classes, the imaginary and the real. Imaginary disease is a picture held firmly by
the objective mind, which causes more or
less physical correspondence. This kind
of disease is often created in total disregard of the laws governing anatomy or
physiology; and is the hardest to cure,
because persons possessed of it hold to it
so persistently that an entire revision of
their mode of thought must be made before
it can be cured. It is not at all infrequent
to have a patient complain of kidney disease, locating the pain and the organs sev-

eral inches below the waist line. The spleen is often supposed to be in the right side of the body, and phantom tumors appear and disappear. But all these mental pictures, if held long enough, create matrices or vortices, and draw into them the elements that will bring finally the actual disease that was at first purely imaginary.''

Psycho-analysis proceeds upon the assumption that a very large number of cases of disease are caused by repression of normal desires, or by disturbances that have occurred in the past life of the individual. In such cases the root of the disease is so concealed, sometimes through years and years, that it must be searched for.

The psycho-analyst is enabled to locate such difficulties, through dreams, or rather through the interpretation of dreams, or by questioning the patient concerning his past life. The well trained analyst must of necessity secure the friendly confidence of the patient to such an extent that the latter will not hesitate to reveal any experience, no matter how intimate.

As soon, as the patient has been led to remember a particular experience, he is encouraged to talk about it in detail and thus it is brought up from subconsciousness. The analyst then shows him what has been causing the difficulty and when the cause is eradicated it can do no more harm.

It is exactly parallel to a foreign substance in the flesh; there is a horrible swelling, with inflammation, pain, and suffering; the surgeon is called, removes the difficulty, and nature does the rest. The psychological law follows the same procedure. If there has been any abnormal activity, any festering sore in the subconscious mind, going on for years and years, if it can be located by a process of mental analysis and put out of the mental complex and shown to the patient, the catharsis is complete.

Dr. Hugh T. Patrick, clinical professor of nerves and mental disease in Northwestern University Medical School, mentions several interesting cases.

"In many cases of functional nervous disorders the factor of fear is quite obvious. But in many cases, though equally important, it is not at once apparent. Of the latter there are numerous varieties which may be divided into groups. One group embraces patients known to have physical courage. A few years ago there was referred to me one of the most noted as well as fearless men in the ring, a man who was peculiarly carefree, if not careless. He was suffering with what were considered rather vague and baffling nervous symptoms, principally insomnia, lack of interest, and moodiness. A careful analysis soon revealed that some trifling symptoms, due to high living and domestic friction, had served to put the idea into his head that he was losing his mind. This phobia was sickness, and the fear so possessed his soul that he was good for nothing until he got rid of it. Needless to say, the patient himself was quite unconscious of the nature of his trouble, and his physician had overlooked it."

So they could not cure the trouble from a physical standpoint. The situation had to be mentally analyzed, and the cause of the fear dragged out from subconsciousness and exposed to the man. When he had a look at it, why, it had exactly the same effect as pulling an eyelash out from an inflamed eye and letting you see it. Your troubles are all over right away, because you are very sure the disturbing cause has been removed, and you forget about it then.

"A sheep rancher of Wyoming complained of insomnia, loss of appetite, abdominal distress, general nervousness and inability to look after his ranch. What really was the matter with him was fear of cancer of the stomach. This phobia completely unnerved him and caused him to enormously magnify every bodily sensation. But was he a nerveless coward? Decidedly not. There was a time when the cattlemen of the Far West made sheep raising a hazardous occupation. Through these dangerous years he lived without a tremor, though he never went to sleep without a rifle by his side. Once he was informed that three cattlemen had started out to 'get him,' and the information was correct. He mounted his horse and, properly armed, rode out to meet them. As he expressed it, he 'talked them out of it,' and the three would-be assassins turned and rode away. In this encounter he was not in the least apprehensive or uncomfortable, and I learned of the incident only in a conversation about his business.''

He had plenty of physical courage, but when something in the inner organism seemed to be wrong, he was scared. As soon as this doctor discovered what the fear was, he probably produced an X-ray or something of that nature to show the patient that there was nothing the matter. Then drawing the patient's attention to the groundless fear, the doctor was able to convince the patient of the groundlessness of his fears.

"A policeman, 49 years old, suffered from intractable insomnia, head pressure, general nervousness and loss of weight. He was not a man to suspect of fear. For

many years he had been in active service
in one of the worst precincts of Chicago,
and on account of his familiarity with
criminals was frequently sent after the
worst types. He had been in numerous
'gun' fights. Once a notorious 'gunman'
standing beside him fired point blank at his
head. All this disturbed his equanimity
not a whit. And yet his illness was the result of fear pure and simple. It came
about in this way; a malicious person had
preferred against him charges of miscon-
duct, and he was cited to appear before
the trial board. This worried him greatly.
Innocent he keenly felt the disgrace of the
accusation and feared that he might be
suspended or even discharged. He trem-
bled for his well-earned good name and
for his home, on which there was a mort-
gage. Naturally he began to sleep poorly,
to have queer feelings in his head, and then
to feel uncertain of himself. At this junc-
ture some friends sympathetically told him
that one could go insane from worry. These
were the steps: Fear of disgrace, fear of
financial collapse, fear of insanity. But

did the patient know all this? Not he. He knew only that he was nervous, and that he suffered, that he did not feel sure of himself."

When that was dragged out of his consciousness and shown to him as a root of his trouble, and a physician was able to assure him that fear was all in the world that was the matter with him, he made up his mind that he had better give that up. Then he was healed.

The subconscious mentality is sick in a chronic way; it has been made sick by some kind of a mental experience—usually of many years standing—and the sickness is a result of its continuing to cherish that experience and keeping it before itself. This constitutes what is technically called a "running sore" in the subconsciousness —that is, mentally not physically.

A woman had suffered from general debility for a number of years, and had been unable to secure relief; the psychologist began to probe, to see what the trouble was. He began to pronounce words—just anything that came into his thoughts: ''desk, book, rug, Chinaman.'' When he pronounced the word ''Chinaman'' the woman appeared startled, and he asked her what the word ''Chinaman'' suggested to her and why it startled her. The woman said that when she was a little girl, she with a playmate, used to play around a Chinese laundry, that they used to plague the Chinaman by throwing pebbles at him through the open door; that one day the Chinaman chased them with a big knife, and that they were nearly scared to death. ''Yes,'' said the psychologist, ''that is one of the things that I wanted to know.'' Then he began to pronounce more words, presently the word ''water,'' and again the woman was startled. It developed then that one time when she was a very little girl, she and her brother were playing on the wharf and that accidentally she pushed him into the water and he was drowned. She said it was many years ago, when she was a mere child. He said: ''Do you think of these things very often?'' She said: ''No, I do not know that I have thought of them before in fifteen or twenty years." "Well," he said, "I will tell you what I want you to do." (She was at that time in a sanitarium, under the care of a nurse.) "I want you to tell the nurse every day that experience about the Chinaman and also the experience about your brother, and I want you to keep telling it until you have told it so many times that you do not feel bad about it any more; then, see me again in two or three weeks." She did as he directed, and at the end of sixty days she was well. The effect of telling it so often was its becoming commonplace to the conscious mentality, without touching the feelings. So the suggestion then went down to the subconsciousness that it did not feel badly about the incident any more, and the conditions of fear which had persisted for twenty or twenty-five years were erased, and the complex in the subconsciousness was no longer in evidence.

The subconscious mind has perfect memory and is fully equipped at birth. Every child inherits certain characteristics from its ancestors. These are carried in the subconscious mind and brought into play when the life or health of the individual requires them.

It is natural to be born without pain, to develop without pain, to live without pain, and to die without pain. This is as natural as it is for a tree to blossom and bear fruit, which at the proper time drops off without distress. The subconscious will take care of every situation; even when it is interfered with it has a remedy available for every situation. Again, you forget something, but the subconscious mind has not forgotten; as soon as the conscious mind dismisses the matter, it comes to us.

Every engineer knows what it is to sleep over a problem; while he is asleep the subconscious is working it out; or he may lose an article, get excited and anxious about it, and not be able to find it; yet as soon as the conscious mind gives it up and lets go, the sense of where it is comes without effort.

Again there is a difficult situation in your affairs, if you can only persuade your conscious mind to let go, to cease its anxiety, dismiss its fear, give up the tenseness and struggle, the subconscious will ordinarily bring about prosperity. The tendency of the subconscious is always toward health and harmonious conditions. To illustrate, you are in the water over your depth, you cannot swim, you are sinking. If the moment the life guard approaches, you grab him around the neck and impede the action of his arms and limbs, he may be unable to do anything with you, but if you will simply trust yourself in his hands, he will get you out. And so it is absolutely certain that subconscious will be present in every difficult situation and that it will tend to play life guard in your favor, if you can but persuade your consciousness to cease its anxiety, to dismiss its fears, to give up the tenseness of the struggle.

Suppose the conscious mind suffers itself to become angry over every trifle.

Every time it gets angry the impulse is transferred to the subconscious. The impulse is repeated again and again, each time it is stirred up. The second record of anger is added to the first, the third to the second, and the fourth to the third. Soon the subconscious has acquired the habit, and before long it will be difficult to stop. When this situation develops the conscious mind will be subject to the irritating influence from without and the habitual impulse from within. There will be action and reaction. It will be easier to be angry and more difficult to prevent it. Yet every time the conscious mind gets angry an additional impulse will be given to the subconscious, and that impulse will be an additional incentive to get angry again.

Now then, anger is an abnormal condition, and any abnormal condition contains within itself the penalty, and this penalty will be promptly reflected in that part of the body which has the least resistance. For instance, if the person has a weak stomach, there will be acute attacks of indigestion, and eventually these will become chronic. In other persons, Bright's Disease may develop; in another, rheumatism; and so on.

It is evident therefore, that these conditions are effects, but if the cause be removed the effect will vanish. If the individual knows that thoughts are causes, and conditions are effects, he will promptly decide to control his thoughts. This will tend to erase anger and other bad mental habits; and as the light of truth gradually becomes clear and perfect, the habit and everything connected with it will be erased, and the accumulated distress destroyed.

What is true of anger, is true of jealousy, of fear, of lust, of greed, of dishonesty, each of these may become subconscious and each of them eventually result in some diseased condition of the body, and the nature of the disease indicates to the trained analyst the nature of the cause which was responsible for the condition.

Frederic Pierce tells us in "Our Unconscious Mind":

"It is a matter of common observation that everyone is in greater or less degree suggestible. The reaction to suggestion may be either positive or negative, either an acceptance or heightened resistance. In this we see a censorship. An epidemic of a certain type of crime shows, on the part of the perpetrators, imitative response to suggestion implanted both by the elaborate descriptive accounts in the newspapers, and by the great amount of discussion of the outrages, heard on all sides.

"Primitive effects of great intensity are aroused; they break through the primary cultural censorship (which is weak in the criminally disposed person), accumulate energy by being dwelt on in consciousness, and finally become sufficiently strong to surmount all fear of punishment and to control the conduct.

"The remainder of the social group, having a higher cultural censorship, reacts to the same suggestion negatively, and discharges the energy of whatever primitive effects have been aroused, in the form of wrath and the desire for punishment of the criminals."

In this connection, it is interesting to note that one often hears the desire for vengeance expressed in terms of much greater primitive violence than the crime itself actually showed. Psycho-analysts hold that this is a method by which the individual is reinforcing his own none too strong censorship of his Unconscious.

Mind in itself is believed to be a subtle form of static energy, from which rises the activities called "thought," which is the dynamic phase of mind. Mind is static energy, thought is dynamic energy—the two phases of the same thing.

—Walker.

Tradition whispers that in the sky is a bird, blue as the sky itself, which brings to its finders happiness. But everyone cannot see it; for mortal eyes are prone to be blinded by the glitter of wealth, fame, and position, and deceived by the mocking Will-o-the-Wisp of empty honors. But for the fortunate ones who seek with open eyes and hearts, with the artlessness, simplicity and faith, which are richest in childhood, there is an undying promise; and to them the Blue Bird lives and carols, a rejoicing symbol of Happiness and Contentment unto the end.

PSYCHOLOGY.

The observation and analysis, knowledge and classification of the activities of the personal consciousness, consisting of the science of psychology, has been studied in colleges and universities for many years, but this personal or conscious, self-conscious mind does not by any means constitute the whole of the mind.

There are some very highly complex, and very orderly activities going on within the body of a baby. The body of the baby, as such, cannot induce or carry on those activities, and the conscious mind of the baby does not know enough to even plan them or be aware of them. Probably also in most cases there is no one around the baby who even remotely understands what is going on in this highly complex process of physical life; and yet all those activities manifest intelligence, and intelligence of a very complex and high order.

257

From the examination of what goes on
in the human body, from all the complex
processes, the beating of heart and digestion of the food, the secretion and excretion
of the glands, it is apparent, that there is
in control an order of mentality which has
a high degree of intelligence, but it is the
mentality which is operating in the millions of cells which constitute the body,
and so operate below the surface of what
we term consciousness. It is therefore,
subconscious.

The subconscious mind, again assumes
two phases. Connected with each human
person there is a subconsciousness which
may in some sense be regarded as the subconsciousness of that person, but which
merges at a still deeper level into what
may be termed Universal subconsciousness, or into cosmic consciousness. That
may be illustrated in this way: If you
will think of the waves on the surface of
Lake Michigan, insofar as they are above
the level of the troughs, as standing for so
many personal mentalities; and then, if

you will think of a small body of water not
rising above the surface, but in some degree running along with each wave and
merging indistinctly at the bottom into
the great unmoved mass below, which may
be thought of as the deepest level, then
those three levels of the water in the lake
may illustrate to you personal consciousness or self-consciousness, personal subconsciousness, and universal subconsciousness or cosmic consciousness. Now, out of
cosmic consciousness springs personal subconsciousness, and out of that in turn, or
in connection with it, rises personal consciousness.

At the beginning of the experience of the
child, its government is almost wholly
from subconsciousness, but as it goes on,
it becomes aware maybe unconsciously, but
still in a degree aware of the presence of
laws of consciousness which manifest as
justice, truthfulness, honesty, purity, liberty, loving-kindness, and so on, and begins
to relate itself to them and to be governed
by them more and more.

The first thing to note is that, while this mental action is going on continuously, we are normally quite unconscious of it. For this reason it is known as the subconscious department of the mind to distinguish it from that part which functions through the senses of which we are conscious, and which we call the self-conscious. The existence in the body of two distinct nervous systems, the cerebro-spinal and the sympathetic, each with its own field of operation and its special functions, prepared us for these two mental departments.

The cerebro-spinal system is used by the self-conscious and the sympathetic by the subconscious. And just as we find in the body that, while the functions and activities of the two nervous systems are different, provision has been made for very close inter-action between the two, so we will find that, while the functions and activities of the two mental departments are different, there is a very definite line of activity between them.

The main business of the subconscious mind is to preserve the life and health of the individual. Consequently it supervises all the automatic functions, such as the circulation of the blood, the digestion, all automatic muscular action and so on. It transforms food into suitable material for body building, returning it to conscious man in the form of energy.

Conscious man makes use of this energy in mental and physical work, and in the process uses up what has been provided for him by his subconscious intelligence.

The action of the subconscious is cumulative and may be illustrated in the following manner. Suppose you take a tub of water and begin to stir it with a small piece of wood from right to left, with a circular motion. At first you will start only a ripple around the wood, but if you keep the wood in motion with the circular movement, the water will gradually accumulate the strength which you are putting into the wood, and presently you will have the whole tub of water in a whirl. If you were then to drop the piece of wood, the water would carry along the instrument that originally set it in motion, and if you were suddenly to stop the wood while it is still projecting in the water, there would be a strong tendency to not only carry the wood forward, but to take your hand along with it. Now, suppose that after you have the water whirling, you decide that you do not want it to whirl, or think that you would prefer to have it whirl in the other direction, and so try to set it going the other way, you will find that there is great resistance, and you will find that it will take a long while to bring the water to a standstill, and a still longer time before you get it going the other way.

This will illustrate that whatever the conscious mind does repeatedly the subconscious will accumulate as a habit, any experience which the subconscious receives is stirred up and if you give it another one of the same kind it will add that to the former one and so keep on accumulating them indefinitely, the tendency being to accumulate activity along any definite line in increasing measure, and this holds true concerning any phase of activity that comes within range of human consciousness. This is true whether the experiences are for our benefit or otherwise, whether the experiences are good or evil. The subconscious is a spiritual activity and spirit is creative, the subconscious therefore creates the habits, condition and environment which the conscious mind continues to entertain.

If we consciously entertain thoughts associated with art, music and the aesthetic realm, if we consciously entertain thoughts associated with the good, the true and the beautiful, we shall find these thoughts taking root in the subconsciousness and our experiences and environment will be a reflection of the thought which the conscious mind has entertained. If, however, we entertain thoughts of hatred, jealousy, envy, hypocrisy, disease, lack or limitation of any kind, we shall find our experience and environment will reflect

the conditions in accordance with these
thoughts: "As we sow, so shall we reap,"
the law is no respecter of persons; we
may think what we will, but the result of
our thoughts is governed by an immutable
law. "There is nothing either good or
evil, but thinking makes it so." We cannot plant seed of one kind and reap fruit
of another.

Consciousness consists in the power to
think, to know, to will and to choose, self
consciousness is the power to be aware of
the self as a thinking, knowing, willing
and choosing individual. The brain is the
organ of the conscious mind and the cerebro-spinal nervous system is the system of
nerves by which it is connected with all
parts of the body.

The process of growth is a subconscious
process, we do not carry on the vital processes of nature consciously, all the complex processes of nature, the beating of
the heart, the digestion of food, the secretion of the glands require a high degree
of mentality and intelligence. The personal consciousness or mind would not be

capable of handling these intricate problems, they are therefore, controlled by the Universal Mind, which in the individual we call the subconscious.

The Universal Mind is sometimes referred to as the Super-Conscious, and sometimes the Divine Mind. The subconscious is sometimes called the subjective and the conscious the objective mind, but remember that words are simply the vessels in which thought is carried. If you get the thought you will not be concerned about the terms.

Mind is a spiritual activity and spirit is creative, hence the subconscious mind not only controls all the vital functions and processes of growth, but is the seat of memory and habit.

The sympathetic nervous system is the instrument by which the subconscious keeps in touch with the feeling or emotions, thus the subconscious reacts to the emotions, never to the reason, as the emotions are much stronger than the reason or intellect; the individual will therefore frequently act in exactly the opposite manner from what the reason and intellect would dictate.

It is axiomatic that two things cannot occupy the same space at the same time. What is true of things is true of thoughts. If, therefore, any thought seeks entrance to the mental realm which is destructive in its nature, it should be quickly displaced by a thought which has a constructive tendency. Herein lies the value of a ready made affirmation, such as the Coue affirmation, "Day by day, in every way, I am growing better and better," or the Andrews' affirmation, "I am whole, perfect, strong, powerful, loving, harmonious and happy." These or similar affirmations may be committed to memory and repeated until they become automatic or subconscious. As physical conditions are but the outward manifestations of mental conditions, it will readily be seen that by constantly holding the thought expressed in the affirmation in the mind, that it will be but a comparatively short time until conditions and environment begin to change so as to be in accordance with the new method of thinking.

This same principle can be brought into operation in a negative way, through the process of denial. Many make use of this with excellent results.

The conscious and subconscious are but two phases of action in connection with the mind. The relation of the subconscious to the conscious is quite analogous to that existing between a weather vane and the atmosphere. Just as the least pressure of the atmosphere causes an action on the part of the weather vane, so does the least thought entertained by the conscious mind produce within the subconscious mind, action in exact proportion to the depth of feeling characterizing the thought and the intensity with which the thought is indulged.

It follows that if you deny unsatisfactory conditions, you are withdrawing the creative power of your thought from these conditions. You are cutting them away at the root. You are sapping their vitality.

The law of growth necessarily governs every manifestation in the objective, so that a denial of unsatisfactory conditions will not bring about instant change. A plant will remain visible for some time after its roots have been cut, but it will gradually fade away and eventually disappear, so the withdrawal of your thought from the contemplation of unsatisfactory conditions will gradually but surely terminate these conditions.

This is exactly an opposite course from the one which we would naturally be inclined to adopt. It will therefore have an exactly opposite effect to the one usually secured. Most persons concentrate upon unsatisfactory conditions, thereby giving the condition that measure of energy and vitality which is necessary in order to supply a vigorous growth.

> The stars come nightly to the sky;
> The tidal wave comes to the sea;
> Nor time, nor space, not deep, nor high,
> Can keep my own away from me.
> —John Burroughs.

METAPHYSICS.

Creation consists in the art of combining forces which have an affinity for each other, in the proper proportion, thus oxygen and hydrogen combined in the proper proportions produce water. Oxygen and hydrogen are both invisible gases but water is visible.

Germs, however, have life; they must therefore be the product of something which has life or intelligence. Spirit is the only Creative Principle in the Universe, and Thought is the only activity which spirit possesses. Therefore, germs must be the result of a mental process.

A thought goes forth from the thinker, it meets other thoughts for which it has an affinity, they coalesce and form a nucleus for other similar thoughts; this nucleus sends out calls into the formless energy, wherein all thoughts and all things are held in solution, and soon the thought is clothed in a form in accordance with the character given to it by the thinker.

269

A million men in the agony of death and torture on the battlefield send out thoughts of hatred and distress; soon another million men die from the effect of a microbe called "the influenza germ." None but the experienced metaphysician knows when and how the deadly germ came into existence.

As there are an infinite variety of thoughts, so there are an infinite variety of germs, constructive as well as destructive, but neither the constructive nor the destructive germ will germinate and flourish until it finds congenial soil in which to take root.

All thoughts and all things are held in solution in the Universal Mind. The individual may open his mental gates and thereby become receptive to thoughts of any kind or description. If he thinks that there are magicians, witches or wizards who are desirous of injuring him, he is thereby opening the door for the entrance of such thoughts, and he will be able to say with Job, "The things I feared have come upon me." If, on the contrary, he thinks that there are those who are desirous of helping him, he thereby opens the door for such help, and he will find that "as thy faith is, so be it unto thee' is as true today, as it was two thousand years ago.

Tolstoi said: "Ever more and more clearly does the voice of reason become audible to man. Formerly men said: 'Do not think, but believe. Reason will deceive you; faith alone will open to you the true happiness of life.' And man tried to believe, but his relations with other people soon showed him that other men believed in something entirely different, so that soon it became inevitable that he must decide which faith out of many he would believe, reason alone can decide this."

Attempts in our day to instill spiritual matters into man by faith, while ignoring his reason, are precisely the same as attempts to feed a man and ignore his mouth. Men's common nature has proven to them that they all have a common knowledge, and men will never more return to their former errors.

The voice of the people is the voice of God. It is impossible to drown that voice, because that voice is not the single voice of any one person, but the voice of all rational consciousness of mankind, which is expressed in every separate man.

Reason tells man that the Universe is a Cosmos, and is therefore governed by law, so that when we see that some persons secure extraordinary results by mental or spiritual methods, reason tells us that we can all do exactly the same thing, because the law is no respecter of persons, and that this is being done every day all the time, everywhere, is apparent to everyone who has taken the trouble to ascertain the facts.

All manifestations are governed by principles which we recognize as universal laws, and in the manifestation of those laws we recognize system, order and harmony.

If the Infinite is omnipresent it must encompass and interfiltrate all that seems to be matter and be one with it and inseparable from it.

Science teaches that so-called matter exists in a diversity of grades from its crudest visible form to the most refined and invisible state in an inseparable relationship with spirit, from which it can never be disassociated.

The latent, or electric, power in the gaseous condition of the elements acts through vibration upon all matter in the combinations lower than the gases by induction, raising them also to a fluidic or gaseous condition and enabling them to form new combinations on a higher plane.

By the same principle is the mineral raised to the sphere of electricity, magnetism, or light, which of themselves are nothing more than ether in different velocities of vibration.

Radio activity consists in setting in motion certain electric vibrations, which after passing through the ether, record themselves on a distant receiver. The whole system depends on the intangible substance known as ether. It is a substance invisible, colorless, odorless, inconceivably rarefied, which fills all space. It fills the space between the earth and the sun and the stars, and it also fills the minute space between the atoms of the densest substance, such as steel. Even when electricity passes through a wire it is merely a vibration of the ether which circulates between the atoms composing the copper wire.

In turn we have abundant proof of the subjugation of Ethereal Matter by the still more rarefied sphere of force which we recognize as Psychic Force or Mind Force.

Matter thus refined becomes the plastic associate of the mind for the transmission of its forces in the manifestation of its power.

That mind does transmit its forces through, or by, its vibrations, we have proof of in the expression of its power of mind over mind, as in the manifestation of the mind of the hypnotist over his subject through mental suggestion, by which he is enabled to control the entire organism of his subject to such an extent as to suspend the functions of the organs of the body at will.

Thus we see that the subtle or refined elements of matter at the disposal of the mind are subject to his control. Matter in itself has no consciousness or feeling, and is active only when controlled by spirit or mind in accordance with the laws that govern its action, and when active gives forth the manifestation and power of the spirit, mind, or intelligence behind it, and acting upon it; and in its varied manifestations symbolizes the wisdom or intelligence of the mind of man, or of the Infinite Mind itself.

As the Infinite Mind rules and governs the Universe, so it is ordained for man to rule and govern his living Universe which he has created or evolved, known as "The Temple of the Living God," an abridgment or Microcosm of the Universe of the Infinite.

Wisdom is the proper use of knowledge to bring about harmony, happiness, ease and health. Ignorance is the darkness which the light of truth disperses, which light alone can enable us to understand the priority of mind in the control of matter.

The office of metaphysics is to bring man into a true comprehension of his relationship with the world, in which he lives, moves, and has his being, and an understanding of how to gain dominion over all which is his rightful heritage.

The metaphysician gives the patient nothing which he can see, nothing which he can hear, nothing which he can taste, nothing which he can smell and nothing which he can feel. It is therefore, absolutely impossible for the practitioner to reach the objective brain of the patient in any way whatever.

It will be said that he may give a mental suggestion; he may send him a thought. This might be possible if it were not for the fact that we do not consciously receive the thoughts of others except through the medium of the senses.

Again, admitting that it might be possible to reach the conscious mind without the aid of any material agency, the conscious or objective mind would not receive it because the objective mind is the mind with which we reason, plan, decide, will, and act. The practitioner invariably suggests perfection, and such a thought would be instantly dismissed by the objective mind as contrary to reason and therefore unacceptable, so that no result would be accomplished.

The Mind which the metaphysician calls into action is the Universal, not the individual. Their formula is: "Divine Mind always has met and always will meet every human need." This Divine Mind is the creative principle of the Universe. It is the "Father" which the Nazarene had in mind when he said: "It is not I that doeth the work, but the Father that dwelleth within me. He doeth the work."

It will at once become apparent that this power which the metaphysician utilizes is spiritual, not material; subjective not objective. For this reason it becomes necessary to reach the subconscious mind instead of the conscious mind. Here then is the secret of the efficacy of the method. The sympathetic nervous system is the organ of the subconscious mind. This system of nerves governs all of the vital processes of the body—the circulation of the blood, the digestion of food, the building of tissues, the manufacture and distribution of the various secretions; in fact the sympathetic nervous system reaches every part of the body. All vital processes are carried on subconsciously. They seem to have been purposely taken out of the realm of the conscious and placed under the control of a power which would be subject to no change or caprice.

The subjective mind, the subconscious mind, the Divine Mind, are therefore simply different terms of indicating the "One mind in which we live and move and have our being." We contact this mind by will or intention. Mind is Omnipresent, we may therefore contact it anywhere and everywhere, neither time or space require consideration.

As spirit is the Creative Principle of the Universe, a subjective realization of this spiritual nature of man, and his consequent perfection, is taken up by the Divine Mind and eventually manifested in the life and experiences of the patient.

Some will say that this ideal state of perfection is never realized. To be sure, the Great Teacher anticipated this criticism for did He not say: "In my father's house are many mansions?"—indicating that there are many degrees of perfection; that although the law operates with immutable precision, the operator may be uninformed or inexperienced. The ability to throw the thought up and beyond the evidence of the senses into the realm of the uncreate, where all that ever was or ever will be, is waiting to be brought forth, to be organized, developed, and crystalized into tangible form, is not the work of the enthusiast who has just come into the knowledge of his spiritual inheritance. It is rather the work of one who has become responsive to the most subtle vibrations, he who can hear the Voice of the Silence, he who has come into the terrible realization that the oasis he saw as he passed over the desert was but a mirage, and as he approached, it receded; he who is no longer astonished or amazed to find that after all, real power is impersonal, that it may make a super-beast of one and a super-man of another.

A great many do not understand the Principle of Metaphysics and the method of applying it so as to work intelligently in their own behalf. Under such conditions they can only expect to rely on some one else, and when that is done continually or at frequent intervals, it tends to weaken rather than strengthen the spiritual factor in consciousness.

It is, therefore, desirable and necessary to secure an understanding of the nature of Truth. Most persons who have become interested in Metaphysics have had some wonderful experience or they know of some one who has had such an experience.

It has been declared by philosophers, religionists, and scientists, again and again, that no proof of the existence of the absolute Truth is possible, in other words that the only way in which a man can be convinced of the creative power of Truth is by demonstration, or by assuming that Truth is all powerful and then on the basis of this assumption make the demonstration. This is *proof,* this is freedom, this is why it has been said: "Ye shall know the truth and the truth shall make you free."

Observation of the characteristic manifestations of anything and deductions based upon such observation, constitute knowledge of that thing; it will readily be seen, therefore, that, if you have observed and have become aware of the fact of certain characteristic manifestations of Truth, you will have knowledge. If it should come to pass that you had observed and carefully noted *all* the characteristic manifestations of Truth, and then in addition perceived the uniformities that run through those manifestations, especially if they are complex, and see the laws or system upon which their characteristics are based, then your knowledge of Truth would be complete.

Through the mental and spiritual awakening of a century ago, which was responsible for modern progressive thought, certain higher forces and principles were
discovered in the mind of man; and in the
same way new realms of thought and spiritual reality were opened to consciousness
—revelations, literally, that gave life a
changed and marvelous meaning, and that
caused the cosmos to extend into infinity,
seemingly, in every direction. And therefore a two-fold purpose appeared at the
very beginning of this movement—to know
the Real Man, and to know the Real Cosmos; an ancient desire, but which was re-
born at this time, and with so much life
and virility that it has become today a
soul passion in the minds of millions.

What then are the characteristics of
Truth? All agree that in the philosophical
sense Truth is that which is absolute and
changeless. Truth must then be a fact;
what then is a fact? Well, three times three
equals nine. That is a fact, always was
a fact, always will be a fact; there can be
no evasion, no argument, no equivocation.

It is truth in the United States, in China, in Japan, it is true everywhere; all the time. A fact exists in the nature of things without beginning, without end, without limitation, it governs our actions and our commercial operations. Those who would undertake to disregard it, would do so at their peril. It is, however, a fact which you cannot see, you cannot hear, you cannot taste, nor can you smell or feel it, it is inapprehensible to any of the physical senses; is it therefore, any less a fact? It is without color, size or form; is it for this reason any less true? It is without years; is it for that reason not the same yesterday, today, and forever?

You may use this fact as long as you live, millions of other persons may use it as often as they like, that will not destroy it. Use does not change it; from everlasting to everlasting—three times three equals nine. This is therefore a fact or the Truth.

Truth is the only possible knowledge which man can possess, because knowledge which is not based upon truth would be false, and would therefore, not be knowledge at all.

Counterfeit money is not true money, it is false, however much it may pass for true. The Truth is therefore, all that any one can know, for what is not true does not exist, therefore we cannot know it. We all think we know much that is not so, but what is not so, does not exist, therefore we cannot know it.

Therefore, the Truth or absolute knowledge is the only possible knowledge and any other use of the word is not scientific or exact.

The metaphysicians of the East will not give out spiritual knowledge miscellaneously. They will not give it to children or young people except under conditions when they have them directly under control and directly under instruction as definitely as we have our children under instruction, in the intellectual life in our schools.

In India when a young man is to be initiated into things spiritual, a definite seven years' course is provided for him under a master, and he is given first the things that he first ought to know along these lines. He is forewarned with regard to dangers that may arise, and the whole course of his journey is guarded by his master with the greatest care, so as to prevent his stumbling during the early stages.

If spiritual metaphysics becomes popular in our Western world, the same thing will develop here. People will not take up the most advanced work, before becoming acquainted with the simpler forms of knowledge. Attainment implifies obligation, if you are somewhere up the ladder of culture, if you have entered the school of understanding, if you have seen the light of spiritual Truth, you are supposed by that very fact to know more than the one who has not yet arrived. Your nervous system will automatically organize itself on a higher plane, and because of this you must live closer to the law of your being or experience suffering more quickly; there are no exceptions to the law.

The resurrection from the dead is not a process of getting corpses out of the grave, it is the elevation of mentalities from the plane of the material to the plane of the spiritual, it is crossing the river Jordan and entering the "Promised Land." It is not until one becomes acquainted with the laws governing in the spiritual world that he really begins to "live," consequently those who are still functioning in the material world are "dead," they have not yet been resurrected. "Eyes have they but they see not, ears have they but they hear not."

Those who have been raised to the spiritual plane, find that there are many practices which they must drop, in most cases these practices leave the individual without difficulty, they drop away of their own accord, but when the individual persists in functioning in the old world, he usually finds that: "A house divided against itself will not stand," and frequently must suffer severely before he learns that he cannot violate spiritual laws with impunity.

PHILOSOPHY.

Physical Science has resolved matter into molecules, molecules into atoms, atoms into energy, and it has remained for Mr. J. A. Fleming, in an address before the Royal Institution, to resolve this energy into mind. He says: "In its ultimate essence, energy may be incomprehensible by us except as an exhibition of the direct operation of that which we call Mind or Will."

We find, therefore, that science and religion are not in conflict, but are in perfect agreement. Mr. Leland makes this quite plain, in an article on "World Making." He says: "First, there is wisdom that has planned, and so adjusted all the parts of the universe in such a perfect balance that there is no friction. And as the universe is infinite, the wisdom that has planned it must be infinite, too.

287

"Secondly, there is a will that has fixed and ordained the activities and forces of the universe, and bound them by laws inflexible and eternal. And everywhere this Omnipotent Will has established the limitations and directions of the energies and processes, and has fixed their everlasting stability and uniformity.

"And as the universe is Infinite this Will must be Infinite.

"And thirdly, there is a power that sustains and moves, a power that never wearies, a power which controls all forces; and, as the universe is Infinite, the Power must be Infinite, too. What shall we name this Infinity trinity, Wisdom, Will and Power? Science knows no simpler name for it than God. This name is all embracing."

We can conceive something of its meaning, though we cannot comprehend its significance. And this Being is the indwelling and ultimate. He is imminent in matter as in spirit; and to Him all Law, Life, Force, must be referred. He is the sustaining, energizing, all-pervading Spirit of the universe.

Every living thing must be sustained by this Omnipotent Intelligence, and we find the difference in individual lives to be largely measured by the degree of this in telligence which they manifest. It is a greater intelligence that places the animal in a higher scale of being than the plant, the man higher than the animal; and we find this increased intelligence is again in- dicated by the power of the individual to control modes of action and thus to con- sciously adjust himself to his environment. It is this adjustment that occupies the at tention of the greatest minds and this ad- justment consists in nothing else than the recognition of an existing order in the Uni- versal Mind, for it is well known that this mind will obey us precisely in proportion as we first obey it.

As we increase in experience and de- velopment, there is a corresponding in- crease in the exercise of the intellect; in the range and power of feeling, in the ability to choose, in the power to will, in all executive action, in all self consciousness. That would mean that self-consciousness is increasing, expanding, growing, developing, and enlarging; it increases and develops because it is a spiritual activity; we multiply our possession of spiritual things in proportion to our use of them. All material things are consumed in the using. There is a diametrically opposite law governing the use of the spiritual and the material.

Life is that quality or principle of the Universal energy which manifests in so-called organic objects as growth and voluntary activity, and which is usually co-existent in some degree, with some manifestation of that same Universal Energy as the quality or principle termed intelligence. There is only one Supreme Principle, evading all comprehension of its essential nature. It is the Absolute. Man can think only in terms of the relative. Therefore, he sometimes defines it as the Universal Intelligence, the Universal Substance, as Ether, Life, Mind, Spirit, Energy, Truth, Love, etc. His particular definition at any moment is governed by the particular relationship of the phenomena of Being in which he thinks of this Principle at that moment.

Mind is present in the lowest forms of life, in the protoplasm, or cell. The protoplasm, or cell, perceives its environment, initiates motion and chooses its food. All these are evidences of mind As an organism develops and becomes more complex, the cells begin to specialize, some doing one thing and some another, but all of them showing intelligence. By association their mind powers increase.

Whereas in the beginning each function of life and each action is the result of conscious thought, the habitual actions become automatic or subconscious, in order that the self-conscious mind may attend to other things. The new actions will, however, in their turn, become habitual, then automatic, then subconscious in order that the mind again may be freed from this detail and advance to still other activities.

Until very recently, it was said that matter, in its ultimate nature was eternal, though all the forms thereof change. We were told that a building destroyed by fire with nothing but a few ashes left had gone up in smoke and gas, and that only the form of the manifestation had changed; that the essential substances were still in existence in different chemical formations.

We were told that all forms of matter exist in the form of·molecules, that these molecules are resolvable into certain smaller elements called atoms. Until recently the atom was supposed to be the ultimate particle of matter, so until recently scientists supposed that matter could be resolved into atoms and that was final.

But with the discovery of radium, it was found that the atom is made up of a large number of smaller particles called electrons or ions, and these electrons vary according to the kind of atom, that is under consideration. A hydrogen atom contains a different number of electrons than an oxygen atom, and so on.

The atoms within the molecule are separated from each other by very great distances as compared with their diameter, the electrons in turn are separated from each other by distances as compared to the diameter, as are the planets in the solar system. When we remember that the molecule which is the larger of the group is so small that it cannot be discovered by the most powerful microscope, so small that you could place many millions of them into an ordinary thimble, you can conceive how infinitesimal is the ultimate particle of matter called the electron or ion.

It has been discovered that the atoms of radium are constantly radiating their ions into space, producing what is called radio activity, that these particles are apparently lost, they simply vanish.

Finally it has been discovered that other forms of matter besides radium are throwing off their ions into space, and that these seem to be absolutely lost in the process, thus the atoms of matter are constantly wasting away, so that the modern physicist no longer claims that matter is indestructible; it is in a constant state of flux, it is forever changing in form.

What then is the director which controls the action of the ion, which indicates the form which it is to take? Mind is the director, and this direction is the process called creation.

It will therefore readily be seen that the basis upon which matter rests is mind or spirit. The spirit of a thing is therefore, the thing itself, it is the spirit of a thing which attracts to itself the necessary electrons for its development from the ether, and which are gradually assembled by the law of growth; it is evident therefore, that the saying of St. Paul is true: "The things which are seen are temporal, but the things which are not seen are eternal."

Many years ago, John Bovee Dods, wrote:

"We have mounted from lead up to electricity, and though as we rose, we found each successive substance more easily moved than the one below it, still we have not as yet found a single material that possesses inherent motion as its attribute. Lead, rock, earth, and water are moved by impulse. Air is moved by rarefaction, and electricity is moved by the positive and negative forces. True we have mounted up, as before remarked, to electricity, but even this cannot move, unless it is thrown out of balance in relation to quantity as to its positive and negative forces.

"Electricity is a fluid most inconceivably subtle, rarefied and fine. It is computed to require four million particles of our air to make a speck as large as the smallest visible grain of sand, and yet electricity is more than seven hundred thousand times finer than air! It is almost unparticled matter, and is not only invisible, but so far as we can judge, it is imponderable.

"It cannot be seen — it cannot be weighed! A thousand empty Leyden jars, capable of containing a gallon each, may be placed upon the nicest scale, and most accurately weighed. Then let these be filled with electricity, and, so far as human sagacity can determine they will weigh no more. Hence to our perception a thousand gallons weigh nothing.

"As electricity, in regard to motion stands upon the poise, being completely balanced by the positive and negative forces, that equalize each other, so it is easily perceived, that if we mount one step higher, we must come to that substance whose nature is to move, and the result of that motion is thought and power. It is MIND. Hence it will be distinctly perceived, in view of the argument now offered, that we cannot, as philosophers, stop short of motion in the highest and most sublime substance in being. This conclusion, as the result of argument, is absolutely and positively irresistible, and challenges refutation.

"When we mount up in our contemplations through the various grades of mat-

ter, and see it continually brightening—as
we press onward in our delightful ca-
reer of rapture, until we arrive at that sub-
limated substance which can neither be
seen or weighed; which moves with a velocity of twelve million miles per minute,
and can travel around this globe in the
eighth part of a second,—we are struck
with astonishment and awe! But as this
is not the last link in the immeasureable
chain, we are forced to proceed onward till
we arrive at the finest, most sublime, and
brilliant substance in being—a substance
that possesses the attributes of inherent
or self-motion and living power, and from
which all other motion and power throughout the immeasureable universe are derived. This is the Infinite Mind, and
possesses embodied form. It is a living
being. This Infinite Mind comes in contact with electricity, gives to it motion,
arms it with power, and through this
mighty unseen agent, moves the universe,
and carries on all the multifarious operations of nature.

"Hence, there is not a motion that trans
pires amidst the immensity of His works,
from rolling globes to the falling leaf, but
what originates in the Eternal Mind,
and by Him is performed, through electricity as His agent. Mind is, therefore,
the absolute perfection of all substances
in being; and as it possesses self-motion as
its grand attribute, so it is, in this respect,
exactly the reverse of all other substances,
which are, of themselves, motionless.
Mind, or spirit, is above all, and absolutely disposes and controls all. Hence, Mind
is imponderable—invisible, and eternal.''

SILENCE.

In silence was the Universe conceived,
In silence doth the heart of man seek out
That other heart to rest on; Nature's soul
Yearns ceaselessly to give its speechless calm
    Unto her restless children as they roam
    Far from that central place which is their home

Wouldst know thy Mother Nature face to face?
Wouldst hear her silent heartbeats? Close thine ears
And still thy senses; wouldst thou feel her arms
Enfold thy being? Thou must give thyself
    In uttermost abandon to her will
    That she may teach thee the one truth—be still!

Be still—and from the Silence shall arise
A mem'ry of forgotten mysteries.
A healing peace descending on thy soul
Shall bear it up to regions beyond words
    Where thou shalt learn the secrets of the earth.
    Of wind and flame and how the stars have birth.

Then shalt thou know thy heritage of joy;
Borne on the pinions of the Bird of Life,
Tuned to the rhythm of revolving spheres,
Feeling with all that breathes, with all that strives
    For union with its prototype above,
    The silent comforter whose name is—Love.

                —Frances Poile.

RELIGION.

Destiny is determined, for nations and for individuals, by factors and forces that are really fundamental—such as men's attitude toward one another. Ideals and motives are more potent than events in shaping History. What people think about the abiding concerns of life means more than any contemporary agitation or upheaval.

A few centuries ago it was thought that we must choose between the Bible and Galileo. Fifty years ago it was thought that we must choose between the Bible and Darwin, but as Dean W. R. Inge, of St. Paul's Cathedral, London, says: "Every educated man knows that the main facts of organic evolution are firmly established, and that they are quite different from the legends borrowed by the ancient Hebrews from the Babylonians. We are not required to do violence to our reason by rejecting the assured results of modern research. Traditional Christianity must be simplified and spiritualized. It is at present encumbered by bad science and cari-

300

catured by bad economics and the more
convinced we are of this, the less disposed
we shall be to stake the existence of our
faith on superstititions which are the religion of the irreligious and the science of
the unscientific.''

Modern discontent and unsatisfactory
conditions are the symptoms of a deep
seated and destructive disease. Remedies
applied to these symptoms in the form of
legislation and suppression, may relieve
the symptoms, but they do not cure the
disease which will manifest in other and
worse symptoms. Patches applied to an
old decaying and obsolete garment in no
way improve the garment. Constructive
measures must be applied to the founda-
tions of our civilization and that is our
thought.

A philosophy of life having as its basis
blind optimism, a religion that won't
work seven days a week, or a proposition
that isn't practical appeals to the intelligent not at all. It is results that we want
and to all such the acid test is: Will it
work!

The apparent impossibilities are the very things that help us to realize the possible. We must go over the unbeaten trail of thought, cross the desert of ignorance, wade through the "Swamp of Superstition" and scale the mountains of rites and ceremonies if we ever expect to come into the "promised land of revelation." Intelligence rules! Thought intelligently directed is a creative force which automatically causes its object to manifest on a material plane. Let him that hath an ear to hear, hear!

One of the characteristic signs of a general awakening is the optimism shining through the midst of doubt and unrest. This optimism is taking the form of illumination, and as the illumination becomes general, fear, anger, doubt, selfishness and greed pass away. We are anticipating a more general realization of the Truth which is to make men free. That there may be one man or one woman who shall first realize this Truth in the new era is barely possible, but the preponderance of evidence is for a more general awakening to the light of illumination.

Everything which we hold in our consciousness for any length of time becomes impressed upon our subconsciousness and so becomes a pattern which the creative energy will weave into our life and environment. This is the secret of the power of prayer.

The operation of this law has been known to a few in all ages, but nothing was more improbable than the unauthorized revelation of this information by any student of the great esoteric schools of philosophy. This was true because those in authority were afraid that an unprepared public mind might not be ready to make the proper use of the extraordinary power which the application of these principles disclosed.

We know that the universe is governed by law; that for every effect there must be a cause, and that the same cause, under the same conditions, will invariably produce the same effect. Consequently, if prayer has ever been answered, it will always be answered, if the proper conditions are complied with. This must necessarily be true; otherwise the universe would be a chaos instead of a cosmos. The answer to prayer is therefore subject to law, and this law is definite, exact and scientific, just as are the laws governing gravitation and electricity. An understanding of this law takes the foundation of Christianity out of the realm of superstition and credulity and places it upon the firm rock of scientific understanding.

The Creative Principle of the Universe makes no exception, nor does it act through caprice or from anger, jealousy or wrath; neither can it be cajoled, flattered or moved by sympathy or petition; but when we understand our unity with this Universal Principle, we shall appear to be favored because we shall have found the source of all wisdom and power.

It must be conceded by every thinking person that the answer to prayer furnishes the evidence of an all pervasive, omnipotent intelligence which is imminent in all things and all persons. We have heretofore personalized this ever present intelligence and called it God, but the idea of personality has become associated with form and form is a product of matter. The everpresent intelligence or mind must be the Creator of all form, the director of all energy, the source of all wisdom.

In order to secure the best thought of the world on the value of prayer, "The Walker Trust," recently offered a prize of $100.00 for the best essay on "Prayer." The meaning, the reality and the power of prayer, its place and value to the individual, to the church and the state, in the every day affairs of life, in the healing of disease, in times of distress and national danger, and in relation to national ideals and to world progress."

In response to the invitation 1667 essays were received, they came from every quarter of the globe, they were written in nineteen different languages, the prize of $100.00 was awarded to the Rev. Samuel

McComb, D.D., of Baltimore, Md. A comparative study of these essays is published by the MacMillan Company of New York. In giving his impressions Mr. David Russell of the Walker Trust says: "To practically all the contributors prayer is something real and of inestimable value, but unfortunately there is little information given as to the method by which the law is placed in operation." Mr. Russell, himself, agrees that the answer to prayer must be the operation of a Natural Law, he says: "We know, that to make use of a Natural Law, the intelligence must be able to comprehend its conditions and to direct or control its sequences. Can we doubt that to an intelligence great enough to encompass the spirit, there would be revealed a realm of spiritual law." It seems that we are rapidly coming into an understanding of this law and understanding is control.

The value of prayer depends upon the law of spiritual activity. Spirit is the Creative Principle of the Universe and is Omnipotent, Omniscient and Omnipresent.

Thinking is a spiritual activity, and consists of the reaction of the Individual against the Universal Mind. "I think, therefore I am," when "I cease to think, I cease to exist." Thinking is the only activity which spirit possesses. Spirit is creative, thinking therefore is a creative process, but as the larger part of our thinking processes are subjective rather than objective, most of our creative work is carried on subjectively. But because this work is spiritual work it is none the less real, we know that all the great eternal forces of Nature are invisible rather than visible, spiritual rather than material, subjective rather than objective.

But exactly because thinking is a creative process, most of us are creating destructive conditions, we are thinking death rather than life, we are thinking lack rather than abundance, we are thinking disease rather than health, we are thinking inharmony rather than harmony, and our experiences and the experiences of our loved ones eventually reflect the attitude of Mind which we habitually entertain, for be it known that if we can pray for those we love, we can also injure them by entertaining and harboring destructive thoughts concerning them. We are free moral agents and may freely choose what we think, but the result of our thought is governed by an immutable law; this is the modern scientific phraseology for the Scriptural statement: "Be not deceived for God is not mocked, whatsoever a man soweth, that shall he also reap."

Prayer is thought in the form of a petition, and an affirmation is a statement of Truth, and when reinforced by Faith, another powerful form of thought, they become invincible, because "Faith is the substance of things hoped for, the evidence of things not seen," this substance is spiritual substance which contains within itself the Creator and the Created, the germ, the Elohim, that which enters in, goes forth and becomes one with its object.

But prayers and affirmations are not the only forms of creative thought. The architect when he plans to erect a wonderful new building, seeks the quiet of his studio, calls on his imagination for new or novel features embodying additional comforts or utilities and is seldom disappointed in the results.

The engineer who designs to span a chasm or river, visualizes the entire structure before making any attempt to embody it in form, this visualization is the mental image which precedes and predetermines the character of the structure which will eventually take form in the objective world.

The chemist seeks the quiet of his laboratory and then becomes receptive to the ideas from which the world will eventually profit by some new comfort or luxury.

The financier retires to his office or counting room and concentrates on some problem in organization or finance and soon the world learns of another co-ordination of industry requiring millions of additional capital.

Imagination, Visualization, Concentration are all spiritual faculties, and are all creative, because spirit is the one Creative Principle of the Universe, and he who has found the secret of the creative power of thought has found the secret of the ages. The law stated in scientific terms is, that thought will correlate with its object, but unfortunately the large majority are allowing their thoughts to dwell upon lack, limitation, poverty and every other form of destructive thought, and as this law is no respecter of persons these things become objectified in their environment.

Finally, there is love, which is also a form of thought. Love is nothing material and yet no one will deny that it is something very real. St. John tells us that "God is Love;" again he says: "Now are we all sons of God?" which means that Love is the Creative Principle of the Universe and St. Paul tells us "In Him we live and move and have our being."

Love is a product of the emotions, the emotions are governed by the Solar Plexus and the sympathetic nervous system. It is therefore a subconscious activity and is entirely under the control of the involuntary system of nerves. For this reason it is frequently actuated by motives which are neither dictated by reason or intellect. Every political demagogue and religious revivalist takes advantage of this principle, they know that if they can arouse the emotions, the result is assured, so that the demagogue always appeals to the passions and prejudices of his audience never to the reason. The revivalist always appeals to the emotions through the love nature and never to the intellect, they both know that when the emotions are aroused intellect and reason are stilled.

Here we find the same result obtained through opposite polarities, one appealing to hatred, revenge, class prejudices and jealousy; the other appealing to love, service, hope and joy, but the principle is the same. One attracts, the other repels; one is constructive, the other destructive; one is positive, the other negative; the same power is being placed in operation in the same way, but for different purposes. Love and hatred are simply the opposite polarities of the same force, just as electricity or any other force may be used for destructive purposes just as readily as it may be used for constructive purposes.

Some will say that if God is Spirit and is Omnipotent and Omnipresent, how can He be responsible for destructive conditions; He cannot bring about disaster, want, disease and death. Certainly not, but we can bring these things upon ourselves by a non-compliance with the spiritual laws. If we do not know that thought is creative, we may entertain thoughts of inharmony, lack and disease, which will eventually result in the condition of which these thoughts are the seed forms, but by an understanding of the law we can reverse the process and thereby bring about a different result. Good and evil are thereby seen to be but relative terms indicating the result of our thoughts and actions. If we entertain constructive thoughts only, the result will benefit ourselves or others, this benefit we call good, if on the other hand we entertain destructive thought, this will result in inharmony for ourselves and others, this inharmony we call evil, but the power is the same in either event. There is but one source of power and we can use the power for good or for evil, just as we can make use of electricity for light, heat or power by an understanding of the laws governing electricity, but if we are careless or ignorant of the laws governing electricity, the result may be disastrous. The power is not good in one case and evil in the other; the good or evil depend upon our understanding of the law.

Many will ask, "how does this thought agree with the scripture?" Many millions of Bibles are sold annually, and every discovery in chemistry, science or philosophy must be in agreement with the vital Truth of religious thought.

What then was the thought of the Master concerning the Creator? It will be remembered that the question was put to him by a lawyer: "Master what shall I do to inherit eternal life?" Did He evade the question? Did He quote some ancient authority? Did He recommend some creed or theological dogma? He did not. His answer was direct and to the point: "Thou shalt love the Lord thy God with all thy heart, with all thy soul, with all thy mind and with all thy strength, and thy neighbor as thyself."

Where is this God which the lawyer is told to love? Jesus refers to Him as the Father and when asked concerning Him says: "He that hath seen me hath seen the Father," again "The Father and I are one," again, "It is not I that doeth the work, but the Father that dwelleth in me, He doeth the work," again He taught His disciples to pray: "Our Father which art in Heaven," and when asked concerning the location of Heaven, He said: "Men shall not say Lo here or Lo there, for behold the Kingdom of Heaven is within you." Here then is authority as to the immanence of the Creator, the Father from the Master Physician himself. Thus, we find that Science and Religion are not in conflict and that within the Church and without there is a setting aside of traditional creeds and a return to the things which the Great Teacher taught and the things for which He stood.

The Old Testament has much to say concerning the God of Jacob and of Moses, but this conception of an Anthropomorphic God is principally interesting as indicating the thought of a people who believed that the world was flat, that the sun moved, when science was but magic and religion the dogma of the scholastics.

This was the result of the deductive method of reasoning which originated with certain statements of fact which were universal and absolute, and which were incapable of verification, all other facts must be arrived at by a process of deduction from these original axioms. If facts were observed which seemed to contradict the deductions from which these original axioms were formulated, so much the worse for the facts, they could not be facts. Facts are nothing compared with "statements of Truth" as given by the scholastics. If there were those who persisted in seeing these unwelcome facts, there was the hemlock, or the stake or the cross.

But in the New Testament all of this is reversed, the doctrine of the immanence of God is taught, an objective God is converted into a subjective God, we are told that, "In Him we live and move and have our Being," we are told that "The Kingdom of Heaven is within you," and we are led to infer that God is always in the "Kingdom."

In this connection it is interesting to note that the miscellaneous collection of manuscripts which have finally been put together and called the Bible were written by many different men, of many different locations, and at widely different times. At first these manuscripts were circulated separately, later they were collected into a single volume and for a long time there were serious disputes among the ancient

Jews and the early Church Ecclesiastics as to what manuscripts should have a place in the sacred book. In fact until quite recently there were many of these manuscripts included which are not now to be found in the Bible as recognized by the Protestant Church of today.

The manuscripts comprising the old testament were written originally in Hebrew, those of the new testament in Greek, and not a single original manuscript of any book either of the old or the new testament is in existence today, nor have they been in existence for hundreds of years. We have then only copies of copies of copies many times removed from the original.

When we remember that those who undertook to translate these manuscripts into the English language for the purpose of giving them to the people met with violent opposition, frequently being driven from the country and excommunicated from the church, we see that there was little uniformity in the various translations of these

manuscripts which are now called the Bible
or the "Word of God."

The King James edition which finally
became popular with the people was the
work of fifty-four churchmen who agreed
with each other that all differences of
opinion should be settled at special meet-
ings to be held from time to time and that
all marginal notes concerning the Greek
or Hebrew text should be eliminated. The
fact that this edition had the sanction of
the King was probably the determining
factor in favor of its general adoption, but
aside from this the work came to be held
in high esteem by the scholastics because
of the smoothness and beauty of the dic-
tion, the churchmen who had the revision
in charge evidently sacrificing accuracy
for euphony and rhetoric.

And now we have a strictly "American" Bible, the work of the American Revision Committee in which the famous
definition of Faith by St. Paul, "Now
Faith is the substance of things hoped for,
the evidence of things not seen" is chang-

ed to "Now Faith is the assurance of things hoped for, a conviction of things not seen," from which it would appear that Paul did not begin to have the insight, the vision, the intuition with which he has been credited, the latter translation completely nullifying and destroying what has heretofore been the most wonderful definition of faith ever given to the world.

It will readily be seen that the Nazarene completely reversed the process of thought in vogue at that time, instead of using the deductive method of thinking he used the inductive. He accepted no authority, no dogma, no creed, instead of reasoning from the seen to the unseen, the visible to the invisible, from things temporal to things eternal, He reversed this process completely and as the idea of this immanent God took hold of man, as they began to understand that, "Closer is he than breathing, nearer than hands or feet," then gradually came an awakening, which marks the birth of a splendor such as had never before been known.

If the inductive method of reasoning obtained in religion, we should find all religions co-operating for the purpose of bringing about "Peace on Earth and good will toward men." We should find every school of theology co-operating with every other school for the purpose of spreading the "glad tidings of great joy," telling of a Redeemer who has come "That we might have life and have it more abundantly," and that this abundant life may be had by looking within instead of without. That objective peace is the result of subjective peace, that harmony without is the natural consequence which follows harmony within, that "men do not gather figs from thistles, or grapes from thorns," and that a man's character is the evidence of the value of his religion: "For by their fruits shall they be known," such a religion satisfies the brain as well as the heart, religion is to love justice, to long for the right, to love mercy, to forget wrongs and remember benefits, to love the truth, to be sincere, to love liberty, to cultivate the mind,

to be familiar with the mighty thoughts
that genius has expressed, the noble deeds
of all the world, to cultivate courage and
cheerfulness. To make others happy, to
receive new truths with gladness, to cultivate hope, to see the calm beyond the
storm, the dawn beyond the night. This
is the religion of reason, the creed of science.

The End.

"For we know in part and we prophecy
in part. But when that which is perfect
is come, then that which is in part shall
be done away."

INDEX

SOLAR PLEXUS.
    Location of—53.
    Is brain of—53.
    Function—53.

SPIRIT.
    Creative principle of Universe—44.
    Thought is expression of—87.
    Has neither shape, weight nor color—88.
    Cosmic—92, 93.
    Reasoning is spiritual process—101.

SUB-CONSCIOUS MIND.
    Storehouse of past thoughts—13.
    Is instinctive desire—14.
    Man's organism controlled by—14.
    Great truths hidden in—114.
    Provided with eliminating process—203.
    Constantly receiving messages—203.
    Can be controlled by conscious—204.
    Is director of internal economy—217.
    Never forgets—238, 249.
    Tendency toward health—251.
    Defined—258.
    Assumes two phases—258.
    Main function to preserve life—261.
    Supervises all functions—261.
    Action is cumulative—261.
    Is spiritual activity—263.
    Process of growth is process of—264.
    Known as subjective mind—265.
    Seat of memory and habits—265.
    Reacts to emotion; not to reason—265.

TACT.
    Definition of—110.

TEMPLE OF THE LIVING GOD.
    Defined—275.
THERAPEUTICS.
    Physical plays important part—173.
    Faith in. necessary—173.

Nervous system is instrument of—117.
Is substance of all force and form—120.
Is source of all power and form—123.
No limitations of—123.
Intuition is phase of—131.
Also called super-conscious and Divine Mind—265.

VIBRATION, Law of.
Time and place annihilated—20.
Governs sound, color, heat, etc.—74, 75.
No respecter of persons—85.
All things in nature are modes of—180.
Life and nature vibratory—181.

UNIVERSE, Law of.
Definition of—17.

VISUALIZATION.
Definition of—309.
Is spiritual faculty—310.

VOICE OF THE PEOPLE.
Is the voice of God—272.

WATER.
Chemical combination of—29.
Manifests on three planes—109.
To usher in New Era—143.

WEALTH.
Offspring of power—96.
Ability to produce is source —98.
Product of Labor—137.
Gold supply of world—145.
Not substantial—146.
Is susceptible to power of thought—146.

WISDOM.
Definition of—276.
Is Infinite—276.

REFERENCES AND QUOTATIONS.

S U C C E S S
MAGAZINE CORPORATION
1133 BROADWAY, NEW YORK, N.Y.

May 4th, 1922.

Mr. Chas. F. Haanel,
The Master Key System,

Dr. Mr. Haanel:

I have long wanted to tell you how I appreciate your masterly service to humanity, in teaching people how to tap the great cosmic intelligence and attract therefrom that which corresponds with their ambitions and aspirations. To my mind, no one else has given men and women such valuable help through a correspondence course.

An English tanner, celebrated for the quality of his leather, said that he never could have made such good leather had he not read Carlyle. There are thousands of people in this country who are living better lives and are much more successful in their different lines for having studied the Master Key System.

The Romans used to place statues of their great heroes in public places, where prospective mothers could often see them and imbibe their spirit, because of the influence upon their unborn children. Mothers would also take their young sons to see them, in order to inspire them with the ambition to emulate those heroic characters. I believe that the presence of "The Master Key System" in American homes will have a similar effect in inculcating high ideals in the minds of our youth.

Many people write me for advice regarding the various correspondence courses along practical psychology lines, and I have always taken great pleasure in recommending to them "The Master Key System." Right here I want to add my own testimony of its value to that of the thousands that others have sent you. Personally I have received untold benefits from the course.

It has been some four years since I received this course, and there has scarcely been a month since, in which I have not gone through it. I never take up any of the lessons without finding something new; in fact, the course is a perpetual help and stimulus to me, and I may truthfully say that in many ways you have done for me what the reading of Carlyle did for the English tanner. I have certainly done better work because of the valuable help and inspiration I have received from "The Master Key System," in every page of which I have marked from beginning to end, and punctuated with marginal notes. It is only simply honesty that I should tell you so.

The world needs arousers, awakeners, inspirers more than it needs anything else, and you are among those who are filling this need in a masterly way. "The Master Key System" not only arouses, but it also energizers, keeps one's ambition from sagging. It makes one dissatisfied with a cheap success, dissatisfied with a meagre life, with half-hearted effort, dissatisfied with the lower when the higher is possible.

Phillips Brooks used to say that no one would be willing to live a half life after he had gotten a glimpse of the larger possible self. Everyone who takes your course gets a glimpse of his larger possible life, and an aroused ambition to reach up to it. No one can go through it without feeling a new courage, a new impulse, a new determination to try a little harder to make good; to do something infinitely greater than anything he had ever done before.

No one would be willing to go back to the old order of things after his eyes have been opened to the possibilities of the new order by those mind-awakening lessons. I believe that no one can conscientiously go through them without great uplift and lasting benefit. Though their value cannot be measured by money alone, I may say that, personally, if I could not get another, I wouldn't take a thousand dollars for my course.

With cordial regards and best wishes,

Very sincerely yours,

ORISON SWETT MARDEN,
1133 Broadway, N. Y. C.

NOTE: Mr. Marden is president and editor of Success Corporation and author of many well known inspirational books. Nearly two million copies of his books have already been sold.

YOUTH PUBLISHING CO

New York, N. Y.,
October 29th, 1921.

My Dear Mr. Haanel:—

The English language is inadequate to express my appreciation of your Master Key System. It is indeed a key for those who read it with understanding, for they will find that it unlocks all the good things of life.

All doors of the treasure house of blessings will open to this Master Key. But the preparation of this series of remarkable lessons was not your work alone. You attracted it but you had helpers from the boundless Empire of the Soul.

Only as one is attuned to the harmonies of inspiration can he bring forth and convey to a hungry world such soul satisfying Manna as the Master Key.

My book, "Live and Grow Young," elucidates this and in my new booklet, "The Empire of the Soul," I have endeavored to clearly show the tremendous help to be derived from contact with the source of Truth.

I have been a student of Metaphysics for 35 years, and have never read anything on the subject as clear, comprehensive and helpful as your lessons. May they reach the millions hungering for this illuminating Truth which will banish sickness, bring happiness and the joys of a living life.

Yours truly,
ARTHUR E. STILWELL.

NOTE:—Mr. Stillwell is the builder of the Kansas City and Southern Railroad, the Kansas City Interurban Belt Railroad, Kansas City, Omaha and Eastern Railroad, Kansas City, Mexico and Orient Railroad, Port Arthur Ship Canal. He is the author of "Live and Grow Young," "The Great Plan," "The Light That Never Failed," and other books

THE PRICELESS TREASURE

October 10, 1920.

Dear Mr. Haanel:

Thinking men and women recognize that a new period in the evolution of the race has recently been ushered in.

It is literally true that "old things," old superstitions, old prejudices, age-long barriers, are giving way, and that unrest everywhere is an evidence of the dawning of a new day.

The study of Psychology has been transferred from the text books in the school room to the affairs of every day life, and a marvelous illumination has been cast into the depths of the human mind.

The revelation of the subconscious and its hitherto unknown powers will, in ages to come, be recognized as probably the supreme achievement of the Twentieth Century—if not the supreme achievement of all ages.

The greatest blessing that any human being can ask is the ability to realize his own inherent powers and possibilities, and to make practical use of them.

This ability is worth more to any individual than all the wealth of a Rockefeller, or even the surpassing genius of a Shakespeare.

I venture to say that any intelligent person who will devote his attention systematically to a study of the Master Key System may become the possessor of this priceless treasure.

Yours sincerely,

JAS. W. FREEMAN.

Assistant Editor of Who's Who In America, with offices in Chicago. Mr. Freeman believes that "practical, every-day psychology" is the most promising attempt yet made to interpret human experience, and that it marks the climax of the great teachings of the world—the highest stage that has been reached by man in his search for the Truth.

CHAUNCEY M'GOVERN

"Handwriting Expert"
Documents in Dispute

Hearst Building,
San Francisco, Calif.
Oct. 30th, 1922.

Mons Gaston M de Launay,
Rue de l' Echauderie No. 5,
Reims, Marne, France

Dear Monsieur Launay:

Your letter of enquiry of October 12, 1922, is acknowledged as received this date. In response thereto, let me state:

So great is the number of similar letters, coming to me from all quarters of the globe—India, China, Australia, Africa, as well as Europe, that it would require all of the time of a stenographer to do justice to responses. Hence it is my rule to send each a printed form to state that condition and to refer them to Mr. Haanel himself.

But in view of the distance which your letter has come, and the historic interest attached to the location, I take special pains to write you a personal letter towit:

Everything that I wrote in my published letter to Mr. Haanel is equally true today as it was when first written. Furthermore, my professional commissions have gradually increased until today I am compelled to refuse commissions unless they embrace some feature of special interest to myself, scientifically as well as financially.

Yours Fraternally
CHAUNCEY M'GOVERN.

Austin, Minn., May 3, 1919.

Mr. Charles F. Haanel.
Saint Louis, Mo.

Dear Sir:—

Permit me a word of appreciation for your wonderful Master Key System.

I have been for years a devout searcher for the Holy Grail or Royal Arcana, which would prove the key which would unlock the "Hidden Treasure." I have studied philosophy, ancient and modern; you have synthesized the wisdom of the East and West and given it in a manner so logical and penetrating that by its aid one is able to distinguish wisdom from sophistry, truth from delusion, spiritual expression from psychic vagaries and the sublime operations of spiritual insight and intuition from deceptive visions and false revelations.

Also I have been a student of Mythology and have viewed the Myths of all ancient races or sacred allegories of the deepest spiritual insight from which to gather by symbol, metaphor and parable the cosmic history of the universe and the soul history of mankind; but your meta-physical elucidation and application have made substance of the shadow.

Again I have studied the Mystics from the great teachers whose message has been of universal import and transcendental significance; but found your system to be free from any craving for sensational phenomena, imposition of the credulous or material occultism. You seek the deeper mysteries of mind and soul, rather than those of the astral or material realms. You are arousing the dormant higher mind and making a clear way to the inner sanctuary.

You have successfully taken the mystery out of Mysticism and placed all propositions in the clear light, so that, "He who runs may read."

I consider you a true benefactor to the world

Yours sincerely,

C. H. GIBBONS.

Fourteen-twenty Tampico Avenue,,
Los Angeles, Calif.

Dear Friend:

Socrates, also Plato, his disciple, each held that
the great purpose of philosophic teaching was, to
lead the mind of the inquirer to the discovery of
Truth rather than to Dogma. I firmly believe the
Master Key System of lessons were devised to serve
this same end and purpose.

"Knowledge is power," but "just knowledge" is evi-
dently insufficient to enable humanity to realize the
end and purpose of Life. Conditions prevailing in
the world today prove that something is lacking. It
cannot be a lack of power,—of a kind—then what is
lacking? Neither Church, College, School nor Institution, so far as we can ascertain by a study of
available records, have yet enabled their students to
discover what is wanting.

It will surely be conceded that Perfect Happiness
can only come through "The Perfect Way," and it
would seem that Christianity either lost or missed
something vital during the past; also that the Religions of the world are equally deficient, for humanity is, and has been for several thousand years, just
drifting, without chart or compass, waiting for de-
liverance from they know not what.

It would therefore appear to me after an experience of over fifty years, that we must look outside
of Sectarianism or Partisanship for the Wisdom and
Understanding of which the world is in such dire
need. Consequently, I have sought diligently of late
years, hoping to find what I earnestly believed must
be in existence and available to the Truth Seeker.
I have many times realized my nearness to the goal,
which it was my sincere and earnest aim ultimately to
reach, only to realize on each occasion, there was still
something lacking. At last, I believe that I can cry
out with Archimedes, "Eureka, Eureka." The Master
Key System.

Yours sincerely,
JOHN Y. NORTON.

January 19, 1922.

Mr. Charles F. Haanel,
709 Pine Street,
Saint Louis, Mo.

My dear Mr. Haanel:

Truth reaches all men alike, and is no respecter
of persons, as is demonstrated by the letters you have
from men in prison cells, in universities of note, in
all the professions, and from the timid, struggling
atoms of humanity who have followed the light into
the open road of cherished desire. Each experience
is different, but I am sure you find an equal satisfaction in all. For myself, I have not words to express my appreciation for the treasures shining
through every page of your storehouse of gems.
Each word scintillates and burns itself to the center of one's being, and, no matter how learned he
may be, no matter what his philosophy or religion,
his education or ignorance, there is a note of un-
impeachable finality that grips the mind and calls
forth the verdict, "True, Well-done, Comprehensive,
Concise, Satisfying."

My estimate of your philosophy would be incom-
plete if I failed to mention the courtesy I find in all
your dealings with your patrons. Every inquiry receives prompt attention, and when adjustments have
been necessary or change of address requested each
received as much interest and attention as the first
inquiry concerning the Master Key. Every detail
has been finished under the observance of the fine
courtesies that have so signally marked your dealings; no least thing has been omitted and the last
lesson is finished with profit, and regret that the story
is so short.

LUELLA F. PHELAN.

August 11, 1920.

Mr. Chas. F. Haanel,
St. Louis, Mo.

Dear Mr. Haanel:—

Words are too weak to express the thoughts I would convey. I was led to take up this course of study at a time when I was passing through the darkest hours of my life, physically, mentally, financially, and spiritually. I seemed to have reached the depths of despair. The study has given me a "new lease on life" in each of the states.

It has brought into my life something for which I had blindly been reaching for twenty years, but I knew not where to find it. The affirmations for health have made me well and strong in body.

The new understanding of Life has led from a condition that bordered on insanity to one of mental tranquility.

Financially it has brought me into conditions which I could not have believed possible. In this particular, I have put the teachings of the course to the extreme test, and have realized everything that I visualized.

In expressing my gratitude to you for the many hours of deepest thought which this course made possible, I desire to add the sincere wish that your reward may be commensurate with the great service you have rendered humanity.

I am, most gratefully yours,

MRS. ANNA TWEEDY.

Union, Oregon,
Dec. 22, 1921.

Mr. Chas. F. Haanel,
St. Louis, Mo.

Dear Mr. Haanel:—

Part 23 on money consciousness has been read by me for the fifth time; and prompts me to write these so inadequate words, because there are no words coined in any language that can convey the import of any part of the Master Key. The exposition of the conflict between labor and capital, rich and poor, is so scientifically and so simply put forth that only the brain with no receptive cells can refuse to accept the evidence of its truth.

As in all other questions that I was so sure that I was right and therefore so radical, but especially the rich and poor question, I find that I was radical but radically wrong.

The Master Key has made a discontented, hateing attitude in me into a contented, harmonious, loving and happy man. I would not sell my knowledge that I found in the store house of the Universal and unlocked with your Master Key, for all the gold that there is, because I could not enjoy it without this knowledge.

Yours with love,

JOHN B. HUNTER.

Represa, Calif.,
February 8, 1922.

Mr. Chas. F. Haanel,
709 Pine Street,
St. Louis, Mo.
Dear Mr. Haanel:

I have been both student and teacher of orthodox Theology, Philosophy and Ancient History, combined with a perfect knowledge of over a dozen ancient and modern tongues, and three complete world tours, at one time caused me to think that I had all the knowledge necessary for anyone to have. I had enough education and was optimist enough to know that somewhere, some place, there was some heretofore hidden power that caused all that "is," and that a persevering search for it would perhaps locate it.

Need I tell you of my studies of Confucius Brahma, Buddha, Mohammet, Plato, Artistotle, and Darwin? Also all known religions from Shintoism, Drindism, and all the Christian Churches? Through this I learned that in a combined knowledge of Metaphysics and Psychology, and its use was all that fifteen years of travel, search and study had failed to reveal to me.

Since taking up your Master Key Course, I have come to understand many things that I did not know. I have learned the Natural Laws—the Law of Compensation, and the Law of Cause and Effect. I have found an at-oneness between the Creator and His created that no Theology has ever taught. The Master Key embraces all religions, all philosophies and all knowledge. It is so simple that it cannot fail to be understood, and I hope to see it printed in all languages and used in every school in the world.

Thanking you for your kindness and wishing you every success, I remain, sincerely yours,
GEORGE L. DAVIS.

Ramona, California,
April 8, 1922.

Dear Mr. Haanel:—

The value of a statement depends upon the training and experience of its author. I have six University degrees. The last, Master of Philosophy, was conferred when I was 30, and in the 24 years which have followed, my work has been scientific research, United States engineer, teacher, lecturer and author.

For me your course presents the "Things worth while" in all of them. An outline of all Truth, the knowledge of which required 40 years of study and research on my part, and the average man can make your thoughts his own by a study of your lessons for six months if he will use his God-given powers and follow your instructions.

I have enjoyed the Master Key greatly; the arrangement is most ideal, leading the student step by step, hinting at what is to follow, but giving time for brain cells to grow and be ready to receive the Truths so fully presented. Pure English, thoughtful, definite, concise, not one intimation of levity. Only a Master Mind can hold a student's attention on great and noble thoughts for six months without some diversion.

In mathematics the stupendous possibilities of the "Fourth Dimension" held my attention. In chemistry the structure of atoms and the rearrangement of their component electrons. In psychology may my "seventh degree" diploma represent the untold powers of the human mind when used in co-operation with the Subconscious Mind.

The Fellowship card will recall the unity with the Thinkers who are to create a New Order of life and things, and make of this world a place of which the Creator can say, "It is very good."

Sincerely yours,
ANDREW L. STROUP

City of St. Paul
DEPARTMENT OF EDUCATION
Bureau of Public Schools.

January 19th, 1923.

Mr. Charles F. Haanel,
707 Pine Street,
St. Louis, Mo.
Dear Sir:

I wish to express my sincere appreciation of your wonderful course in psychology. I feel that it is the most useful study anyone can take up as a help in business as well as social life. I can frankly say that it has given me more satisfaction than anything I have ever studied.

The truth of the principles you expound in this course are self evident and as marvelous as the radio is today; in fact the Radio seems to be easily compared with the operations of the mind, for when the radio instrument is tuned in harmony with the sound waves sent from a broadcasting station, one can clearly distinguish the messages sent without material contact. In the same way the individual resembles a radio instrument which needs but to be tuned to receive the vibrations of life and power constantly issuing from the Universal Mind.

Compare a child to the radio instrument and you will find the same principle. As soon as the brain cells are developed enough to faintly distinguish the intelligence of the Universal Mind, the child receives consciousness. Consciousness develops greater consciousness by tuning the mind to more perfect harmony with the Universal Mind which pervades all.

Your course tells the world how to receive the intelligence of the Divine Mind which is all knowing, all power, and present everywhere. It gives the individual the formula for tuning the mind in harmony with the Mind of the Creator and by acquiring this knowledge one can overcome all barriers to success, happiness and prosperity.

I congratulate you and thank you most sincerely.

Yours faithfully,
FRANK A. LETHERT.

The Master Key System

Is the only clear, concise, comprehensive, definite, exhaustive, distinctive, original and scientific presentation of

The Law of Causation

Ever Formulated By

Any One At Any Time.

It is a system of Philosophy embracing the ultimate principles, elements, causes and laws that underlie and explain all knowledge and existence, arranged in an orderly and scientific manner, giving it unity and completeness.

RFG. U. S. PAT. OFF.

The Results

Accruing from the operation of this Principle, are so startling as to appear incredible to the uninitiated. For this reason there are to-day more students of

The Master Key System

than of all similar systems of philosophy combined. The

Price and Terms

Upon which the work is being distributed will be made known upon application.

Charles F. Haanel,

707-709-711 Pine St.
St. Louis, Mo.

LaVergne, TN USA
02 October 2009
159771LV00004B/21/A